Identifying the Characteristics of Fetal Alcohol Spectrum Disorders (FASD) among
Children with Attention-Deficit/Hyperactivity Disorder

A DISSERTATION
SUBMITTED TO THE FACULTY OF THE GRADUATE SCHOOL
OF THE UNIVERSITY OF MINNESOTA
BY

Fumio Someki

IN PARTIAL FULFILLMENT OF THE REQUIREMENTS
FOR THE DEGREE OF
DOCTOR OF PHILOSOPHY

Asha K. Jitendra

April 2011

UMI Number: 3450914

Dissertation Publishing

ProQuest LLC
789 East Eisenhower Parkway
P.O. Box 1346
Ann Arbor, MI 48106-1346

Acknowledgements

The reason I decided to pursue my Ph.D. in the US was my desire to help as many children with special needs as possible in Japan. All the children I worked with brought me here. Every time I struggled, I thought of them, and they always gave me the energy to move forward. Working with these children is such a rewarding job, and I hope that I can share this feeling with many people possible through this dissertation. I also hope that this study will help as many kids in need as possible.

I came to Minnesota all by myself. I never visited here, knew nobody, and actually, I had hardly heard about this place. I could not have gotten where I am now without my friends' help. Bryan Cichy, my very first friend in Minnesota, helped me not only academically, but also emotionally. He listened to my poor English without getting frustrated, took me to his hometown, and taught me about the US culture. Without him, I could not have survived my first year, for sure. Christine Peper, Jason Wolff, and everyone else in the 8701 seminar class have been with me throughout the first half of the entire program. We worked in the same study group for stats classes, took a research methods class together, prepared for the hardest-ever prelim together, and sometimes went out for a drink after the finals were over. With their encouragement and support, I knew I could jump over all the hurdles of graduate school. Mary Beth Kelley, my good friend and also an instructor who assigned me as a "super TA," taught me many things. She taught me how to teach, how to be positive when I got stuck, and how to swear when I feel like it. Naomi Shinoda, my best roommate, supported me through good diet (i.e., cooking for me) and editing all my dissertation chapters. Living with her was really fun. We went grocery shopping together, yoga classes together, and visited our friends together. She always soothed me just by being around me.

Kit Hansen and Kirsten Jamsen, who are wonderful writing consultants, showed me not only how to write using correct grammar but also how to write cohesively and concisely. Meeting them regularly helped me to pace my writing, and what helped me the most was their interests in my topic. Without them, I would never have finished this program.

Dr. Asha Jitendra, my adviser, taught me to always have the highest possible expectations through her attitude towards her own work. I feel very fortunate to be her student. Dr. Pi-Nian Chang, who introduced me to children with fetal alcohol spectrum disorders (FASD), has changed my life. I truly appreciate his generosity to let me do the practicum at the Pediatric Specialty Clinic and allow me to collect data there. Without him, this dissertation would not exist. Dr. Frank Symons and Dr. Matthew Burns helped me since my first year at the University of Minnesota. I appreciate their support, especially when I was struggling to find my career goals and the dissertation topic. Dr. Jill Flower and Dr. Steve Hermann encouraged me and taught me how to cope with stress, which is one of the most important skills I needed to survive in academia.

Nikolas Stavrou, my love, always supported me. He was the person who drew out my potential to the fullest. He encouraged me when I lost confidence, cheered me up when I was sad, and celebrated with me when I got over hurdles. He never doubted my capability to pursue the Ph.D. program, which meant a lot to me. Mr. and Mrs. Stavrou, his parents, were also always so good to me. They treated me as if I was their daughter, and I truly feel that the Stavroues are my second family.

Lastly, I would like to thank my parents, who have been supporting me as much as they can by any means. They have never stopped believing my abilities and my potential. I am very proud and feel fortunate to be their daughter. I love you, mom and dad.

Abstract

Fetal alcohol spectrum disorder (FASD), characterized by various levels of dysmorphia and behavioral and cognitive dysfunctions, is the result of prenatal alcohol exposure. FASD characteristics can be masked by many other conditions. As a result, early identification of FASD is often difficult, leading to a delay of children with FASD receiving necessary services. However, screening children with attention-deficit/hyperactivity disorder (ADHD), which is the major comorbid disorder of FASD, may enable the identification of children with FASD earlier than screening all children in schools. Therefore, the purpose of this study was to examine the differences between children with ADHD only and children with FASD and ADHD in terms of adaptive functioning, behavioral characteristics, and academic performance that impact school outcomes and can be recognized in classrooms. This study conducted a review of the medical records of 149 individuals with single ADHD diagnosis and 189 individuals with dual diagnosis of FASD and ADHD (M_{age} = 11.25, SD = 2.12). Results of analysis of covariance analysis indicated: (1) no difference in adaptive functioning between the dual diagnosis group and the single diagnosis group, (2) the dual diagnosis group exhibited significantly more externalizing behaviors than the single diagnosis group, but the difference between the two groups regarding internalizing behaviors was not significant, (3) there was no significant differences between the two groups on reading and mathematics. Differences in characteristics between the two groups and implications for future research are also discussed.

Table of Contents

Chapter 1

Chapter 2

Chapter 3

Chapter 4

Chapter 5

List of Tables

Chapter 3

Chapter 4

Chapter 1

Introduction

Fetal alcohol spectrum disorder (FASD) is characterized by various levels of dysmorphia and behavioral and cognitive dysfunctions due to prenatal alcohol exposure (Institute of Medicine, 1996). Although this disorder is preventable, it remains the largest cause of mental retardation (i.e., cognitive disabilities; Friend, 2010). Every year, more than 500,000 fetuses (approximately 13% of all births) are exposed to alcohol during pregnancy in the United States (Centers for Disease Control, 2002). Among these children who were exposed to alcohol during pregnancy, approximately 10 per 1,000 live births have some form of FASD (May & Gossage, 2001). FASD poses a significant issue in today's society. The appearance rate of FASD is continuing to rise, and the median of estimated costs of FASD is approximately 3.6 million dollars per year in the United States (Lupton, Burd, & Harwood, 2004).

Because of behavioral and cognitive dysfunctions caused by prenatal alcohol exposure, children with FASD need various levels of support such as special education services and medication. Nevertheless, many children with FASD do not receive the necessary support until when their behavior problems become salient during adolescence. Additionally, there is no particular category to serve FASD in special education under the current law, the *Individuals with Disabilities Education Improvement Act* (2004). Although many children with FASD may receive services under the Other Health Impairments category, the number of children who do receive services under this category is still low. If they have a comorbid condition (e.g., mental retardation), they could receive services for that condition, but not all children with FASD have such a comorbid condition. Most children/adolescents with FASD receive services under the

1

category of emotional behavioral disorder at a later age when they begin to exhibit significant behavioral problems due to having difficulties in life.

Because many adolescents with FASD exhibit significant behavioral problems, this population is overrepresented in the juvenile justice system (Fast, Conry, & Loock, 1999). They often have legal issues and are more susceptible to behavior that harms self and others compared to those without FASD. Fast et al. (1999) reported that of the 287 adolescents (aged 12 to 18) in their study who were remanded for a forensic psychiatric/psychological evaluation, 67 (23.3%) had a diagnosis of FASD. If adolescents with FASD could have been diagnosed and received sufficient intervention services earlier, it is possible that they could have fewer legal issues and incidents of problem behavior. Therefore, it is critical that children/adolescents with FASD start receiving necessary educational services as early as possible to remediate their problem behavior. Given that educators are usually the ones who first recognize that children with FASD have educational needs, they can refer these children to medical professionals for further examination. FASD is a medical diagnosis and requires assessments by medical professionals.

To appropriately diagnose and start intervening early with children with FASD, it is critical to raise awareness about FASD among professionals, especially educators, because they are often the first people to recognize the difficulties these children encounter. In particular, focusing on the differences between children with FASD and attention-deficit/ hyperactivity disorder (ADHD; hereafter referred to as the dual diagnosis), and children with ADHD only (i.e., single ADHD diagnosis without prenatal alcohol exposure) could provide potential indicators for identifying children with FASD among children with ADHD at an early age. There are few previous studies that have compared children with FASD and children with single ADHD diagnosis. Furthermore,

2

most studies examined their performance using laboratory tests (e.g., continuous performance test) or individually administered tests (e.g., Wechsler Intelligence Scale for Children, Wisconsin Card Sorting Test). In sum, identifying these children's difficulties in different areas (e.g., cognitive functioning, executive functioning) as measured by the above mentioned tests may be problematic, because it would be difficult to administer such tests to all children with ADHD. Therefore, it is important to focus on areas that educators can recognize and follow-up by screening to examine the differences between these two populations. Educators may be able to detect signs of difficulty children with FASD and ADHD evidence in the following areas: (1) adaptive functioning, (2) behavioral characteristics (e.g., aggressive behavior and rule-breaking behavior), and (3) academic performance (e.g., reading, math, and writing). An emphasis on these specific areas may be important for educators to understand the diverse needs of children with FASD and inform instruction.

Previous research that examined children with ADHD and children with FASD on the three areas mentioned above revealed that both children with ADHD and children with FASD exhibited diminished adaptive functioning (Jirikowic, Olson, & Kartin, 2008; Stein, Szumowski, Blondis, & Roizen, 1995). However, adaptive functioning of children with FASD appeared to be even more impaired, particularly in the interpersonal area, when compared to children with ADHD (Thomas, Kelly, Mattson, & Riley, 1998). When compared to normally developing children, both children with ADHD and children with FASD showed significantly higher externalizing behaviors and comorbidity of disorders pertaining to internalizing behaviors (e.g., mood disorders; Berkeley, 2006; Brown et al. 1991). However, when children with FASD were compared directly to children with ADHD on these behaviors, the results were incongruent. That is, children with ADHD exhibited significantly more internalizing behaviors than children with FASD, whereas

3

children with FASD exhibited significantly more externalizing behaviors than children with ADHD (e.g., Coles et al., 1997; Greenbaum et al., 2009). Regarding academic achievement, both children with ADHD and children with FASD often struggle with core academic subjects (Barkeley, 2006; Coles et al., 1997). However, children with ADHD evidence more difficulties during elementary school, particularly in reading (e.g., Frazier, Youngstrom, Glutting, & Watkins, 2007). In contrast, children with FASD struggle more during adolescence, particularly in mathematics (e.g., Olson, Feldman, Streissguth, Sampson, & Bookstein, 1998).

Research Questions and Hypotheses

The aim of the present study was to examine whether adaptive functioning, behavioral characteristics, and academic performance can be used to identify children with dual FASD and ADHD diagnosis (i.e., the dual diagnosis group) among children with single ADHD diagnosis (i.e., the single diagnosis group). As such, this study explored the following research questions:

(1) What are the differences in adaptive functioning between the dual diagnosis group and the single diagnosis group?

(2) What are the differences in behavioral characteristics between the dual diagnosis group and the single diagnosis group?

(3) What are the differences in academic performance between the dual diagnosis group and the single diagnosis group?

For the first research question, the hypothesis was that although both groups may exhibit difficulties in adaptive functioning, the dual diagnosis group would exhibit more significant difficulties in the area of socialization. Previous studies have shown that

4

children/individuals with FASD exhibit low levels of adaptive functioning, especially when compared to their cognitive functioning (i.e., IQ) (e.g., Jirikowic et al., 2008; Streissguth, et al., 1991). Furthermore, children with prenatal alcohol exposure exhibit noticeable difficulties in the area of socialization, especially in the interpersonal area (Thomas et al., 1998). Children with ADHD were also known to demonstrate diminished adaptive skills, often in the low-average to borderline range, despite having average intelligence (e.g., Barkley, Fischer, Edelbrock, & Smallish, 1990; Stein et al., 1995).

For the second research question on behavioral characteristics, the hypothesis was that the single ADHD diagnosis group would exhibit significantly more internalizing behavior, but the dual diagnosis group would exhibit significantly more externalizing behavior. With regard to internalizing behavior, two studies reported that children with single ADHD diagnosis exhibited significantly more problems in internalizing behavior than children with FASD (Coles, et al., 1997; Greenbaum, Stevens, Nash, Koren, & Rovet, 2009). However, the findings on externalizing behavior, which is the major characteristic of both ADHD and FASD, were contradictory. On the one hand, Coles et al. (1997) reported that children with single ADHD diagnosis exhibited significantly more problems in externalizing behavior on the child behavior checklist (CBCL). On the other hand, Greenbaum et al. (2009) reported that there were no significant differences between the two groups based on parental report. Moreover, educators reported children with FASD exhibited significantly more externalizing behavior than children with single ADHD diagnosis. Children with FASD also exhibited significantly more behavior problems on the Social Skills Rating Scale based on both parental and teacher report.

For the third research question, the hypothesis was that the dual diagnosis group would perform significantly lower on mathematics but perform significantly higher on reading. For example, Coles et al. (1997) compared children with FASD whose

5

ADHD status was unreported and children with ADHD who did not suffer from prenatal alcohol or drug exposure and found that children with FASD scored significantly lower on mathematics assessments, whereas children with single ADHD diagnosis scored significantly lower on reading assessments. Other research indicated that although children with FASD were able to read, write, and count numbers, they had difficulty with calculation and estimation skills (Kopera-Frye, Dehaene, & Streissguth, 1996). In contrast, children with ADHD exhibited the most difficulty in reading, followed by mathematics, and then spelling (Frazier et al., 2007).

Chapter 2

Literature Review

Fetal alcohol spectrum disorder (FASD), characterized by various levels of dysmorphia and behavioral and cognitive dysfunctions (Institute of Medicine, 1996), is the result of prenatal alcohol exposure. Although the effects of prenatal alcohol exposure on fetus have been described from the time of Aristotle (Abel, 1999), FASD has not been studied extensively. The number of children diagnosed with FASD has been increasing, and as of 2000, stands at about 10 per 1000 live births, which translates into about 40,000 babies per year in the United States (May & Gossage, 2001).

Adolescents with FASD are overrepresented in the juvenile justice system (Fast, Conry, & Loock, 1999). Approximately 60 percent of adolescents and adults with FASD encounter trouble with the law, and 30 percent have alcohol and/or drug-related problems (Streissguth, Barr, Kogan, & Bookstein, 1996). They often have legal issues and are more susceptible to criminal behavior compared to those without FASD. Fast et al. (1999) reported that of the 287 adolescents (aged 12 to 18) in their study who were remanded for a forensic psychiatric/psychological evaluation, 67 (23.3%) had a diagnosis of FASD. Unfortunately, it is very difficult to effectively intervene with this population once they begin to exhibit problem behavior.

Although these children are in need of various levels of support, there is no particular category to serve them in special education under the current law, the *Individuals with Disabilities Education Improvement Act* (2004). Most children/adolescents with FASD receive services under the category of emotional behavioral disorder at a later age when they begin to exhibit significant behavior problems due to having difficulties in life. Thus, it is critical for them to start receiving necessary educational services as early as possible. Educators are usually the ones who first recognize that children with FASD have unique needs and refer them to medical professionals for further assessment.

This chapter presents an overview of FASD, including a description of the essential features, diagnostic criteria, and subtypes of FASD, as well as issues related to early identification of FASD. Next, risk factors and protective factors that affect future outcomes of children with psychopathology (e.g., FASD) are discussed. Finally, previous studies that focused on adaptive functioning, behavioral characteristics, and academic performance of children with FASD are reviewed, particularly in comparison with normally developing children and children with ADHD (attention-deficit/hyperactivity disorder) followed by a discussion of the major scales used to measure these three areas.

Fetal Alcohol Spectrum Disorder (FASD)

Essential Features of FASD

FASD is characterized by a spectrum of dysmorphia and behavioral and cognitive dysfunctions due to prenatal alcohol exposure. Four essential features of FASD (originally referred to as fetal alcohol syndrome or FAS) were first introduced in 1996 by the Institute of Medicine. They included (a) growth deficiency, (b) characteristics of FAS facial phenotype (i.e., upper lip thinness, philtrum smoothness, and smallness of palpebral fissures), (c) central nervous system (CNS) abnormalities (i.e., damage/dysfunctions), and (d) prenatal alcohol exposure (Institute of Medicine, 1996). Typically, physicians or pediatricians who specialize in FASD are the ones who gather evidence of growth deficiency and FAS facial phenotype. CNS abnormalities are determined based on structural damage to the brain, as well as the results of

8

developmental and neuropsychological tests that measure IQ, executive functioning, and behavioral and social development. To meet the criteria for CNS abnormalities, children must exhibit a pattern of developmental behavioral or cognitive abnormalities (e.g., impairment in judgment, complex problem solving, abstraction, metacognition, and arithmetic skills; higher-level receptive and expressive language deficits; disordered behavior).

Subtypes of FASD and Diagnostic Criteria

In 2004, the Centers for Disease Control and Prevention proposed that FASD includes four diagnostic categories: fetal alcohol syndrome (FAS), partial FAS, alcohol related birth defect, and alcohol related neurodevelopmental disorder (Hoyme et al., 2005). In addition, the term fetal alcohol effects (FAE) has been used for diagnosing those individuals who do not meet the diagnostic criteria for FAS. However, the ambiguity of the FAE diagnosis (e.g., Aase, Jones, & Clarren, 1995) has led to the disuse of this term.

The diagnosis of FASD is determined on the basis of a combination of the four essential features: growth deficiency, FAS facial phenotype, CNS abnormalities, and prenatal alcohol exposure (Bertrand et al., 2004). Specifically, growth deficiency is verified with growth retardation in height or weight that is below the 10th percentile. Characteristics of FAS facial phenotype (i.e., dysmorphia) include thin vermillion border (i.e., upper lip), smooth philtrum (i.e., vertical groove in the upper lip), and small palpebral fissures (i.e., the opening for the eyes between the eyelids). Vermillion border thinness and philtrum smoothness is rated from 1 to 5 based on the "Lip-Philtrum Guide" (Astley & Clarren, 1999). A rating of 1 indicates that the formation of vermillion border or philtrum is within the normal range, whereas a rating of 2 or 3 indicates between normal and atypical, and a rating of 4 or 5 is considered dysmorphic. Smallness of palpebral fissures is determined by a criterion of below the 10th percentile based on age and racial norms.

CNS abnormalities (i.e., damage/dysfunction) are determined in several ways. CNS abnormalities related to structure may include small overall head circumference (i.e., below the 10th percentile for those who do not exhibit growth deficiency, or the 3rd percentile for those who exhibit growth deficiency) or observable brain abnormalities (e.g., reduction in size or change in shape of the corpus callosum, cerebellum, or basal ganglia) as assessed by imaging techniques. From a neurological perspective, CNS abnormalities can indicate neurological problems such as seizures that are not due to a potential insult or fever or other soft neurological signs (e.g., problems in coordination, visual motor difficulties). With regard to function, CNS abnormalities can entail a global cognitive deficit (i.e., low IQ) or deficits in three or more specific functional domains such as cognition, executive functioning, motor functioning, attention and hyperactivity, social skills, and other domains (e.g., sensory, memory). Functional problems are measured by standardized measures (e.g., Wechsler Intelligence Scale for Children, fourth edition, Wisconsin Card Sorting Test) and determined based on the norms.

In addition to these three diagnostic criteria (growth deficits, all three facial abnormalities, and CNS abnormalities), confirmed prenatal alcohol exposure is preferred but not necessary for diagnosis of FAS. The criteria for partial FAS consist of at least two facial abnormalities, CNS abnormalities, and confirmed prenatal alcohol exposure (Hoyme et al., 2005). The criteria for alcohol related birth defect are at least two facial abnormalities, more than one congenital structural defect including malformations or displasias (i.e., an abnormality in maturation of cells within a tissue), and confirmed prenatal alcohol exposure (Hoyme et al., 2005). The criteria for alcohol related

10

neurodevelopmental disorder include two or more domain deficits in CNS functioning and confirmed alcohol exposure (Hoyme et al.).

Problems of Early Diagnosis/Identification

Of the four defining features of FASD, growth deficiencies may occur due to many reasons. During pregnancy, prenatal smoking, poor prenatal nutrition, or genetic disorders can lead to growth retardation or deficiencies. After birth, one of the major reasons for growth deficiencies is insufficient nutrition, including the condition stemming from the poor sucking responses of infants (National Center on Birth Defects and Developmental Disabilities, 2004). Thus, it is impossible to identify children with FASD solely by examining growth deficiencies. Additionally, facial phenotype can be masked by birth trauma or other syndromes/disorders (Bertrand et al., 2004; Jones, 1997). CNS abnormalities can be detected at an early age when children with FASD exhibit global cognitive deficit or significant developmental delays, but can be difficult to detect early if cognitive abnormalities are present in areas that require higher-level functions such as executive functions. Lastly, the core feature of FASD - prenatal alcohol exposure - is also hard to detect. If a child is adopted or in foster care, for instance, detailed information about the birth mother, such as presence of prenatal alcohol exposure is not always available. Even if it is possible to interview the birth mother, mothers tend to underreport the levels of drinking during pregnancy (Ernhart, Morrow-Tlucak, Sokol, & Martier, 1988). In general, retrospective interviews about alcohol consumption during pregnancy are not accurate. All these factors make it difficult to diagnose FASD at an early age, which leads to the failure of early intervention to remediate difficulties in the various domains encountered by children with FASD.

Early Identification of Children with FASD

An important aspect of early diagnosis of FASD is adequate referral of children who may have FASD to medical professionals for evaluation. The referral process may require screening children with attention-deficit/hyperactivity disorder (ADHD), a population that overlaps with children with FASD. A recent report revealed that almost 95 percent of children with FASD also have ADHD (Fryer, McGee, Matt, Riley, & Mattson, 2007). As such, there is a high likelihood (95%) of identifying children with FASD by carefully screening children with ADHD. Unfortunately, a lack of awareness about FASD often results in children with FASD being diagnosed as having only ADHD. Some researchers argue that if a child has both FASD and ADHD diagnosis, medical treatment, particularly, needs to focus on FASD, because reaction to medication was reportedly different for children with single ADHD diagnosis and those with the dual FASD and ADHD diagnosis (O'Malley & Nanson, 2002). Although methylphenidate (i.e., stimulants) is known to be effective for children with ADHD (Connor, 2006), O'Malley, Koplin, and Dohner (2000) found that children with FASD responded better to dextroamphetamine (79%) than to methylphenidate (22%). This difference in response to medication suggests that children with single ADHD and those with the dual diagnosis are qualitatively different from a biological perspective.

Developmental Psychopathology

Early identification of children with FASD is critical in order to remediate the specific academic, behavioral, and social problems that they encounter. A theory of developmental psychopathology may serve to explain why early intervention is critical for a good prognosis. Developmental psychopathology, based on the ideas of psychopathology and developmental psychology, is "the study of the origins and course

12

of individual patterns of behavioral maladaption" (Sroufe & Rutter, 1984, p. 265). Psychopathology focuses on the manifestation of causes and course of psychopathology (i.e., mental disorders) to explain why individuals develop mental disorders and the type of pathways a disorder may take (e.g., conduct disorder in childhood often leads to antisocial personality disorder in adulthood). Developmental psychology focuses on an individual's development from infancy to late adulthood, for example (Rutter & Sroufe, 2000). Development is an active and dynamic process, whereby individuals perceive and respond to experiences in their environment. Not only do individuals respond to the various experiences, but also are affected differentially by such experiences (Rutter & Sroufe, 2000).

From a developmental psychopathology perspective, no single starting point (i.e., birth) reaches the same ending point (i.e., outcomes). For instance, monozygotic twins who share the same genetic factors (i.e., starting points) could likely end up with one being a criminal and another a successful business person (i.e., ending points). Outcomes are not only limited to occupation, but also can indicate status such as academic achievement, prosocial and antisocial behavior, and psychopathology. Even when the starting point is exactly the same, there are many pathways individuals may take and various outcomes are possible based on their pathways. Additionally, more than one pathway may reach a particular outcome (e.g., good grades, antisocial personality disorder). The path that an individual takes is often influenced by a combination of both risk and protective factors.

Risk Factors and Protective Factors of Good Prognosis

Risk factors and protective factors are very important when considering prognosis of individuals with psychopathology. While risk factors such as low socioeconomic status

13

(SES), low birth weight, maltreatment, violence, parental divorce, and poor parenting are predictors of poor outcomes, (Maesten & Garmezy, 1985), a combination of risk factors has multiplicative rather than additive effects on outcomes (Streissguth & Kanter, 1997). That is, the effect of one individual holding two risk factors is more than twice the effect of one individual holding a single risk factor. For instance, the overall amount of impact of risk factors on one person with both ADHD and FASD is more than that of the combined impact of the same factors on one person with ADHD or FASD alone. Unfortunately, many risk factors often co-occur (e.g., Maesten & Wright, 1998). Protective factors are on the opposite side of the continuum of risk factors (e.g., good parenting vs. poor parenting), and lowering risks often means increasing protective factors (Maesten, 2001).

Developmental psychopathology perceives comorbidity of disorders either as the result of the same set of intercorrelated risk factors or a sequence of the risk mechanism leading to one form of psychopathology that could result in another form of psychopathology (Rutter & Sroufe, 2000). For instance, hyperactivity and inattention are risk factors for later development of antisocial behavior (Farrington, Loeber, & van Kammen, 1990). At the same time, hyperactivity and antisocial behavior are known to have different developmental paths (Ferguson & Horwood, 1993). That is, hyperactivity in itself is a marker for childhood disruptive behavior, but the persistence of such disruptive behavior leading to antisocial behavior depends not only on hyperactivity but also on other risk and protective factors (Rutter & Sroufe, 2000). In particular, experiences in early life play important roles on later antisocial behavior (Rutter, 1981). As such, having FASD (i.e., psychopathology) is an additional risk factor for children with ADHD. Therefore, identifying the presence of FASD early and providing these children with necessary supports are likely to increase protective factors.

14

Prenatal Risk and Protective Factors of Children with FASD

Abel and Hanningan (1996) listed three major prenatal risk factors of FASD (at that time, FAS): pattern of alcohol consumption, poverty, and smoking behavior. Regarding alcohol consumption, the blood alcohol level threshold for abnormal brain development is about 150 mg/dl (Pierce & West, 1986; Bonthius, Goodlett, & West, 1988). Therefore, drinking seven glasses in a short period of time on weekends is more harmful than drinking two glasses every day, even though the total amount of alcohol consumption per week is the same, because the first situation is likely to exceed the blood alcohol level threshold. The risk can differ based on the mother's race. For instance, African American population has higher incidence of FASD than the Caucasian population (e.g., Sokol et al., 1986, 1989). One possible explanation for this difference is that some females (e.g., African American) have embryo/fetal genotype that is more vulnerable to teratogens (e.g., alcohol) than others (e.g., Caucasian: Christoffel & Salafsky, 1975). Further, a pattern of drinking of females with alcohol problems may differ depending on race. It is known that among females who abuse alcohol, African Americans are more likely to drink heavily on weekends only, whereas Caucasians consume alcohol throughout a week (Dawkins & Harper, 1983). Therefore, even though both African American and Caucasian females may consume the same amount of alcohol in a week, African American females could demonstrate higher blood alcohol levels based on their pattern of drinking, which could lead to a greater risk of abnormal brain development of fetus compared to their Caucasian female counterparts.

A second prenatal risk factor of FASD may be related to poverty. During pregnancy, poor maternal nutrition and health or adverse stress on mothers maybe a function of poverty. Poor nutrition and stress can harm the fetus by increased adrenal

15

release of corticosterone and epinephrine (Abel & Hannigan, 1996). Even after birth, poor nutrition of mothers may lead to malnutrition of infants, especially given that many infants with FASD exhibit poor sucking response (Day et al., 1991). Moreover, mothers who abused alcohol during pregnancy tend to drink after delivery (Jester, Jacobson, Sokol, Tuttle, & Jacobson, 2000), which suggests the high possibility of postnatal alcohol exposure during nursing.

In addition to such physical impacts, emotional impacts may occur. Child maltreatment can pose a serious risk to the well being of the child. Infants/children with FASD are at a high risk of maltreatment, because they are often difficult to raise (Gardner, 2000). Furthermore, mothers' current alcohol use is related to poor family functioning, high occurrence of domestic violence, and low quality of parental intellectual stimulation of children with FASD (Jester et al., 2000). When considering emotional distress, unawareness of FASD often leads to inappropriate treatment of these children. FASD is often described as a hidden disorder due to its subtle dysmorphia and generally good basic language skills (e.g., vocabulary and syntax: Burtrand et al., 2004). Children with FASD may be deemed stubborn and exhibit inappropriate behavior and get reprimanded often than normally developing children.

Smoking is another risk factor that is often observed in alcoholic females (Coles, Smith, Fernhoff, & Falek, 1985). Nicotine is a teratogen that harms a fetus and when combined with alcohol can have an additive or even synergistic effect on the fetus to result in low birth weight, smaller head circumference, and learning difficulties, to name a few (e.g., Wright et al., 1983; Halmesmaki, 1988; Olsen, Pereira, & Olsen, 1991).

Prenatal care of high-risk mothers is one potential means of decreasing the above-mentioned risk factors before birth. Although the occurrence or the severity of FASD can be decreased during pregnancy, it is not always possible. After birth, early intervention can decrease the effect of risk factors and maximize the effect of protective factors for children with FASD. Some known protective factors of children with FASD include a stable and nurturing home environment during the school years, early diagnosis of the disorder (before age 6), having no exposure to violence, and receiving social and educational services (Streissguth, Barr, Kogan, & Bookstein, 1996; Olson, 2002). Furthermore, being in a relatively few foster/adoptive family placements can be considered a protective factor. Some children have experienced multiple foster/adoptive placements or frequently moved from one family member to another (e.g., living with a mother, then grandparents, then a father), and such unstable placements can have a negative impact on children with FASD (Streissguth et al., 1996).

Identifying Children with Single ADHD Diagnosis and Dual Diagnosis

Examining the differences between children with FASD and ADHD (i.e., hereafter referred to as "dual FASD and ADHD diagnosis") and children with ADHD only (i.e., hereafter referred to as "single ADHD diagnosis") could provide potential indicators for early identification of children with FASD among children with ADHD. Few previous studies have compared children with FASD to children with single ADHD diagnosis; however, most studies compared their performance on laboratory tests (e.g., continuous performance test: CPT) or individually administered tests (e.g., Wechsler Intelligence Scale for Children, Wisconsin Card Sorting Test). Given that most individually administered tests are administered by psychologists and schools typically have one school psychologist, identifying these children's difficulties in areas that are measured by the above mentioned tests may be problematic for the following reason. Administering these tests to all children with ADHD would be time intensive and challenging. Therefore, it is important that educators focus on essential areas when referring children for

17

screening of FASD or ADHD. Early indicators of difficulty children with dual FASD and ADHD diagnosis exhibit could include the following areas: (1) adaptive functioning, (2) behavior (e.g., internalizing and externalizing behavior), and (3) academic performance (e.g., reading, mathematics, and writing).

Adaptive Functioning

Adaptive functioning is "the collection of conceptual, social, and practical skills that have been learned by people in order to function in their everyday lives" (American Association on Mental Retardation, 2002, p.14). Adaptive behavior is a collection of skills that are necessary for daily life at home and in the community and may include self-help (e.g., toileting and dressing skills), communication (e.g., understanding directions, appropriately greeting others), motor (e.g., riding a bike, using scissors), and social/community skills (e.g., crossing a road with attention to traffic signals, using social services such as police stations, libraries). Adaptive behavior is age-related, modifiable, defined by surrounding people, and defined by a person's typical performance rather than ability (Sparrow, Cicchetti, & Balla, 2005).

Although several standardized scales of adaptive behavior exist, the ones that are frequently used in research and practice are the Vineland Adaptive Behavior Scales, Second Edition (VABS-II) and the Scales of Independent Behavior - Revised (SIB-R). Both scales can be administered either by professionals as a structured interview or completed by a caregiver. The VABS-II measures four areas, namely communication, daily living skills, motor skills (only for ages under 6), and socialization, which together provide the Adaptive Behavior composite score (Sparrow et al., 2005). The VABS-II also includes the Maladaptive Behavior subscale. The manual reports reliability indices for internal consistency, test-retest reliability, and interrater reliability to be around .80s,

18

which is deemed adequate. Validity indices for criterion validity and factor structure are also reported to be satisfactory.

The Scales of Independent Behavior– Revised (SIB-R) comprise Motor Skills, Social Interaction and Communication Skills, Personal Living Skills, and Community Living Skills clusters (Bruininks, Woodcock, Weatherman, & Hill, 1996). The total scores for each cluster can be converted to the Broad Independence cluster score. Each cluster includes two to five subscales, and each subscale has about 20 items that are rated using a 4-point scoring procedure (i.e., 0 as "never or rarely" to 4 as "always or almost always does very well"). The SIB-R also includes the Maladaptive Behavior index (i.e., Internalized, Asocial, Externalized, and General). Reliability such as internal consistency, test-retest reliability, and interrater reliability are reported to be over .90s, which is strong. Validity, such as criterion validity and construct validity are also reported to be satisfactory.

Adaptive behavior of children/individuals with FASD. Results of previous studies showed that children/individuals with FASD exhibit low levels of adaptive functioning, especially when compared to their cognitive functioning (i.e., IQ) (e.g., Jirikowic et al., 2008; Streissguth, Aase, Clarren, Randels, LaDue, & Smith, 1991). Children with prenatal alcohol exposure exhibit noticeable difficulty in the area of socialization, which starts to appear in childhood (Whaley, O'Connor, & Gunderson, 2001) and persists into adolescence and adulthood (e.g., Olson et al., 1998; LaDue, Streissguth, & Randels, 1992). Within the area of socialization, the interpersonal area is more significantly impaired than the other areas (Thomas et al., 1998). Additionally, verbal IQ is strongly correlated with social abilities (Sattler, 1992) and children with FASD often have low verbal IQ (e.g., LaDue et al., 1992; Rasmussen, Horne, & Witol,

19

2006). The study by Thomas et al. (1998) compared the adaptive functioning of 15 children with FASD (M_{age}= 10.3, SD = 2.0, mean Verbal IQ = 76.8) and 15 children without prenatal alcohol exposure, who were matched on their verbal IQ scores (M_{age}= 9.2, SD = 1.6, mean Verbal IQ = 77.7). Results indicated that children with FASD scored significantly lower than the verbal-IQ-matched controls on Interpersonal and Use of Play and Leisure Time skills, both of which comprise the Social Skills domain of the VABS. Moreover, these statistically significant differences remained even after SES, the only demographic characteristic that was significantly different between the two groups, was controlled. In contrast, no difference was observed between the two groups in the Coping area.

In contrast, Howell, Lynch, Platzman, Smith, and Coles (2006) reported that the VABS scores of 128 adolescents who were exposed to alcohol during pregnancy did not differ from the scores of the 53 nonalcohol exposed adolescents (i.e., control group). Those who were exposed to alcohol were further divided into two groups: dysmorphic (i.e., exhibited growth retardation and/or dysmorphic features) and non-dysmoprhic. The participants in this study did not necessarily have FASD, but their mothers drank at least twice a week during pregnancy. Neither the dysmorphic (N = 46, M_{age}= 15.14, SD = 1.08, mean full scale IQ = 72.35) nor the non-dysmorphic group (N = 82, M_{age}= 14.86, SD = 0.83, mean full scale IQ = 78.37) demonstrated significant differences in adaptive functioning compared to the nonexposed control group.

One plausible explanation for the equivocal results from FASD studies may relate to the inclusion criteria used in the research. Even after 1996, when there was consensus on the diagnosis of FASD, not all researchers used the FASD diagnostic criteria in their research. Many of the studies did not report a diagnosis of FASD for their sample of participants that had been exposed to alcohol during pregnancy. In other words, these participants may have included both children with FASD and children without FASD. Because the diagnosis of any form of FASD requires CNS abnormalities, it is very likely that functioning of children with FASD is more impaired than in those without FASD, even though both groups were prenatally exposed to alcohol. Thus, it is not surprising that those without FASD diagnosis outperform those with FASD diagnosis in various areas.

It must be noted that many of the studies on individuals with prenatal alcohol exposure were large-scale, community-based, long-term follow-up studies (e.g., Streissguth et al., 1996). The recruitment of clinic-referred patients with FASD as participants is usually easier than finding participants in the community. However, clinic-referred patients do not necessarily represent the FASD population as a whole. Thus, research findings about children with FASD may not necessarily reflect the real characteristics of these children.

When interpreting the research findings about adaptive functioning, comorbid (i.e., overlapping) disorders are important factors to consider. Some of the studies included participants with common comorbid disorders of FASD, such as disruptive behavior disorders including conduct disorder (CD) and oppositional defiant disorder. Other studies have excluded particular disorders such as cerebral palsy, autism, and mental retardation (i.e., IQ < 70) that include their own unique characteristics apart from FASD. Despite previous efforts to identify the impact of comorbid disorders on adaptive functioning, it is still unclear. It is known that children with CD, ADHD, language disorders, and depression also demonstrate deficits in adaptive functioning (Manikam, Matson, Coe, & Hillman, 1995; Paul, Looney, & Dahm, 1991; Powell & Germani, 1993; Spelt, DeKlyen, Calderon, Greenberg, & Fisher, 1999; Stein et al., 1995; Vig & Jedrysek, 1995). Whaley et al. (2001) compared the adaptive functioning of 33 clinic-referred

21

children with FASD (M_{age}= 6.15, SD = 2.38, mean full scale IQ = 83.5) and 33 children at the child psychiatry clinic who were not exposed to alcohol prenatally but matched on IQ (M_{age}= 6.15, SD = 2.30, mean full scale IQ = 83.3). Diagnosis of the matched psychiatric group included receptive and expressive language disorders, mental retardation, ADHD, bipolar disorder, major depressive disorder, but not pervasive developmental disorders (e.g., autism, Asperger's syndrome). Results indicated no significant differences between the FASD group and the matched psychiatric group on adaptive functioning. As such, deficits in adaptive functioning may not be a unique characteristic of children with FASD. However, age was a significant predictor of the VABS score, suggesting that impairment in adaptive functioning might become more salient as children with FASD get older.

Another factor to be considered when examining adaptive functioning is SES, which is known to be associated with the level of adaptive functioning (Tucker et al., 1995). In the Howell et al. (2006) study discussed earlier that included both adolescents exposed to alcohol during pregnancy and nonalcohol exposed adolescents, the sample was from low socio-economic families. The mean VABS scores of children with prenatal alcohol exposure were within the average range despite their low SES status. In contrast, the mean scores of nine adolescents with FASD aged 14 to 16 years (mean full scale IQ = 91.1) from middle class families in the Olson et al. (1998) study exhibited poorer adaptive functioning than expected on the basis of their IQ, with mean overall adaptive functioning being almost close to the clinical cut-off score. These children scored relatively worse on Socialization, compared to Communication and Daily Living Skills. Further study is needed to draw a firm conclusion about the relation between the level of adaptive functioning and SES.

22

Adaptive behavior of children/individuals with ADHD. Children with ADHD were also known to demonstrate diminished adaptive skills, often in the low average to borderline range (e.g., Barkley et al., 1990; Stein et al., 1995), despite having average intelligence. The discrepancy between their cognitive functioning (i.e., IQ) and adaptive functioning was about 1.5 to 2 *SD* (Roizen, Blondis, Irwin, & Stein, 1994). Additionally, the level of adaptive functioning was not significantly affected by comorbid conditions of learning disorders or other disruptive behavior disorders (Roizen et al., 1994). This may be a reflection of a discrepancy between knowledge and performance in children with ADHD (Barkley, 2006).

Diminished adaptive skills were still present in adulthood for many individuals with ADHD. When compared to the normal control group, clinic-referred adults with ADHD were more likely to have divorced or remarried and had job-related troubles such as being fired from employment, impulsively quitting a job, or switching jobs frequently (Murphy & Barkley, 1996). However, studies on adults in particular, but more often studies on children or adolescents, include participants that are clinic-referred. As such, results of such studies may indicate more significant difficulties in adaptive functioning than community-based samples.

Behavioral Characteristics

According to Merriam-Webster Dictionary, behavior is "anything that an organism does involving action and response to stimulation" (Merriam-Webster's collegiate dictionary, 2003). It is impossible to directly measure behavior, but we can observe behavior and record it. There are two major ways to assess behavior: direct observation and rating scales (Cohen & Spenciner, 2006). Direct observation is not standardized and is often conducted in naturalistic settings such as classrooms and playgrounds.

Observation can be either qualitative (e.g., anecdotal) or quantitative (e.g., event recording). For research purposes, teacher and/or parent rating scales are frequently used. Unlike individually- or group-administered tests, behavior rating scales are likely reliant on a rater's personal perspective (Cohen & Spenciner, 2006) even though they are standardized. Moreover, some behavior rating scales that are currently available also have problems in reliability or validity (Cohen & Spenciner, 2006). For this reason, detailed information of major behavior rating scales are described below before discussing behavioral characteristics of children with FASD and ADHD.

The Child Behavior Checklist (CBCL) is a standardized rating scale to assess behavioral and emotional problems (Achenbach & Rescorla, 2001). It consists of 118 items to be rated according to three levels (i.e., not true, somewhat or sometimes true, very or often true) and 20 open-ended items about the child's daily life (e.g., hobbies, chores, strengths, weaknesses). The CBCL is a parent rating scale; the teacher rating scale is called the Teacher Report Form (TRF), and the two forms are basically parallel (Achenbach, 1991b). There are also self-rating scales for adolescents (i.e., Youth Self-Report Form). All three of these forms are composed of several components: Externalizing Problems (i.e., Aggressive Behavior and Rule-Breaking Behavior), Internalizing Problems (i.e., Anxious/Depressed, Withdrawn/Depressed, and Somatic Complaints), and Other Problems (i.e., Social Problems, Thought Problems, and Attention Problems). All forms can be either self-administered or administered by an interviewer. Reliability such as test-retest reliability and interrater reliability are reported to be mostly in the middle to upper .90s, which is strong. However, there is a noted discrepancy between mother and father's ratings about their clinic-referred child. Validity, such as criterion validity and construct validity is reported as satisfactory.

The Social Skills Rating System (SSRS) is a rating scale to measure children's

24

social behavior (Gresham & Elliott, 1993). There are parent, teacher and student forms; the parent and teacher forms consist of three composites: Social Skills, Problem Behavior, and Academic Competence. The Social Skills and Problem Behavior items are rated on a three-point scale with 0 as "never" and 2 as "very often." The Academic Competence items are rated on a five-point scale from 1 as "Lowest 10%" to 5 as "Highest 10%." The number of items for each composite is 30, 18, and 9, respectively. With regard to reliability, internal consistency for the teacher form is around the mid .80s, but reliability coefficient for the parent and student are mostly in the .70s and .60s, respectively. These indices indicate that the parent and student forms are not very reliable. The findings are for test-retest reliability, with reliability coefficients in the mid .80s for the teacher and parent forms, but .50s to .60s for the student form. Validity, such as content, criterion-related and construct validity is also relatively low. Based on these facts, the parent and student forms of the SSRS are not suitable for use.

Behavioral characteristics of children/individuals with FASD. Using the CBCL, Olson et al. (1998) examined the behavior of nine adolescents aged 14 to 16 years, (three boys and six girls) who were highly exposed to alcohol during pregnancy. The average T-score of the Behavior Problems for boys and girls were 72.7 (i.e., Clinical range) and 61.2 (i.e., Borderline range), respectively. A T-score of over 63 translates into the Clinical range, and over 60 is the Borderline range. Average scores of both boys and girls appeared higher than scores for boys (mean = 50.4) and girls (mean = 50,0) in the cohort comparison group that was in the average range; however, due to the small number of FASD participants (i.e., nine), statistical analysis was not performed. A longitudinal study conducted by Steinhausen and Spohr (1998) with 27 children with FASD that they followed from preschool to adolescence (M_{age}= 13.08, SD = 1.64) also

25

used the CBCL and its parallel form for teachers, the Teacher Report Form (TRF). Children with FASD (M_{age}= 13.08, SD = 1.64) exhibited social relationship problems, a finding that was congruent with previous research reporting problems in social skills on adaptive functioning scale for these children. In addition to teacher and/or parent report, adolescents with prenatal alcohol exposure have self-reported antisocial behavior (Olson et al., 1997). The work of Brown et al. (1991) found similar results of lowered social competence and elevated externalizing behavior problems in 47 children prenatally exposed to alcohol (M_{age}= 5.66, SD = 0.72 for 22 children whose mother stopped drinking during pregnancy, M_{age}= 5.86, SD = 0.95 for 25 children whose mother drank alcohol throughout the pregnancy) based on teacher report. Moreover, the Steinhausen and Spohr (1998) study revealed that the CBCL and TRF profiles of children with FASD did not change until adolescence. At the initial assessment (i.e., preschool), these children exhibited problem behavior in terms of social and attention skills according to both parental and teacher reports and at follow-up (i.e., adolescence), they continued to exhibit the same problem behavior.

Other studies that examined the behavior of children with FASD used the Social Skills Rating System (SSRS). Schonfeld, Paley, Frankel, and O'Connor (2006) noted that according to parent report, 98 children (51 boys and 47 girls) with some form of FASD (M_{age}= 8.61, SD = 1.5) presented very poor social skills, with the standard scores (SS) well below 1 SD from the mean. In contrast, their social skills were low but within the average range (i.e., SS > 1SD, lower SS means poorer social skills) according to teacher reports. Parent reports indicated that all the children exhibited more problem behavior than average (i.e., SS > 1SD, higher SS means more problem behavior). Based on teacher reports, only children with FAS or partial FAS exhibited more problem behavior on average than children with alcohol related neurodevelopmental disorder

26

(ARND). In sum, although results suggest discrepancies between teacher and parent reports, discrepancies in scores on the Problem Behavior between parent and teacher forms were less than those on the Social Skills.

It is important to note that the reliability of the scale used (i.e., the SSRS), particularly of the parent form, was not very satisfactory. In the study by Schonfeld et al. (2006), most children (79%) lived in an out-of-home placement. As such, these children might not have lived with their parents long enough for their parents to understand their behavior. Therefore, while teacher report may better represent children's behavior, the reliability of teacher ratings is also questionable. For instance, children who exhibit problem behavior tend to experience frequent changes in the educational setting (e.g., from regular classroom with a use of resource room to self-contained classroom, to special school) such that teachers do not know the children well enough to adequately rate their behavior. Additionally, gender is considered a significant predictor of social skill level. Based on both the teacher and parent forms, boys were reported to have fewer social skills than girls and children with FASD exhibited receptive-expressive language disorders that affected their social cognition and social communication skills (Coggins, Friet, & Morgan, 1998).

Using the SSRS teacher form, Jirikowic et al. (2008) reported similar, but different results from the Schonfeld et al (2006) study. Participants were 25 children with FASD (14 boys and 11 girls, M_{age} = 6.5, SD = 0.88), and a comparison group of 26 normally developing children (14 boys and 12 girls, M_{age} = 6.9, SD = 0.85). On the Social Skills, Problem Behavior, and Academic Competence subtest, scores for the FASD group were in the average range (96.8, 108.9, 92.3, respectively). However, compared to the normal control group, children with FASD scored significantly higher (p < .01) on the Problem Behavior. Scores on the other two composites did not differ from scores for the normal control group.

Differences between the mean scores in the above two studies can be explained by participant characteristics. Participants in the Schonfeld et al. (2006) study were mostly clinic-referred and exhibited severe problems in various areas, whereas participants in the Jirikowic (2008) study were recruited from a community-based FASD prevention network. Thus, it is understandable that the average scores of the former group indicated more severe problems than the latter group.

Behavioral characteristics of children/individuals with ADHD. Behavior problems, particularly impulsivity and hyperactivity are the core symptoms of ADHD (DSM-IV-TR; American Psychiatric Association, 2000). To qualify for ADHD diagnosis, behavior problems have to be observed in multiple settings. As such, parent and teacher ratings of their problem behavior (e.g., the Externalizing Problems scores of the CBCL) should be consistent. On the CBCL that includes the component of attention problems, the results of the study by Steinhausen, Metzke, Meier, and Kannenberg (1997) found that children with ADHD scored higher in terms of attention difficulties compared to the normal control group. In fact, given the strong relation between the attention problems and ADHD diagnosis (e.g., Barkley, DuPaul, & McMurray, 1990), a high score (i.e., T-score > 55 to 60) on attention is the most significant item to differentiate children with ADHD from other populations (Chen, Faraone, Biederman, & Tsuang, 1994).

Children/individuals with ADHD often have comorbid disorders. About quarter of these children have conduct disorder (CD), about 35 percent have oppositional defiant disorder (ODD: American Academy of Pediatrics, 2000), and 18 percent of adolescents have some kind of mood disorders (American Academy of Pediatrics, 1996). Some studies revealed that those with ADHD and ODD and/or CD scored higher on the CBCL

28

than those with ADHD alone (e.g., Biederman, Ball, Monuteaux, Kaiser, & Faraone, 2008; Eiraldi, Power, Karustis, & Goldstein, 2000), which was reasonable considering that many of the diagnostic criteria of CD and ODD overlap with the CBCL Externalizing Problems items.

Academic Performance

Performance is "something accomplished" (Merriam-Webster's Collegiate Dictionary, 2003), and thus academic performance entails student accomplishments in academic subject areas. Core subject areas that are often addressed are reading, written expression (including spelling), and mathematics. For the purpose of research, academic performance is measured by individually and/or group administered standardized tests, parent and/or teacher rating scales, or other indicators such as grade point average (GPA), years of retention, and years of education (for adolescents or adults). Many studies on children used individually administered tests and/or rating scales, particularly in core school subject areas. For studies on adults or parental information, an indicator of education level often used is years of education. Brief information about commonly used individually administered achievement tests is provided below.

Individually administered achievement tests that are frequently used in the ADHD and FASD literature are the Wide Range Achievement Test-Revised/Third/Fourth Edition (WRAT-R/3/4), the Woodcock Johnson Tests of Achievement- Third Edition (WJ III ACH), the Wechsler Individual Achievement Test- Second Edition (WIAT-II), and the Arithmetic subtest of the Wechsler Intelligence Scale of Children-Revised/Third/Fourth Edition (WISC-R/III/IV).

The Wide Range Achievement Test-Fourth Edition (WRAT4) is a standardized,

29

norm-referenced achievement test (Wilkinson & Robertson, 2006). The test includes four subtests in the domains of word reading, spelling, mathematics computation, and sentence comprehension. The manual reports reliability such as internal consistency and alternate-form reliability (immediate and delayed retest stability) to be over 0.90, which is strong. Validity (criterion and construct) is also reported as satisfactory.

Woodcock Johnson Tests of Achievement- Third Edition (WJ III ACH) is a standardized, norm-referenced achievement test that includes both the Standard and Extended batteries (Woodcock, McGrew, & Mather, 2001). The Standard battery consists of 12 subtests that measure skills in core academic areas - reading, writing and mathematics. Two of the12 subtests measure memory skills. The Etended battery consists of 10 subtests that measure additional skills (e.g., vocabulary) or in other content areas (e.g., social studies). Reliability indices reported in the manual are range from 0.80s to 0.90s for each subtest, and in the .90s for cluster scores, which is strong. Validity measures, such as criterion validity and construct validity, are also reported as satisfactory.

The Wechsler Individual Achievement Test- Second Edition (WIAT-II) is a standardized, norm-referenced achievement test (Wechsler, 2001). It consists of the Reading, Mathematics, and Written and Oral Language scales. Reliability such as internal consistency or test-retest reliability is reported as ranging from mid .70s to mid .80s, which is moderately satisfactory. Validity, such as criterion validity and construct validity are also reported as relatively satisfactory.

Some researchers used the Arithmetic subtest of the Wechsler Intelligence Scale of Children-Revised/Third/Fourth Edition (WISC-R/III/IV) to measure overall mathematics achievement (Wechsler, 2003) because this subtest includes various levels of simple word solving problems. WISC-IV is reported to be highly reliable and valid as a

30

comprehensive assessment scale; however, one subtest, the Arithmetic subtest, may not represent children's mathematics achievement very well. The Arithmetic subtest is given orally and test takers are not allowed to take notes. Thus, the results may largely depend on working memory capacity, which is one of the most significant weaknesses in children with FASD (e.g., Streissguth, Barr, & Sampson, 1990; Burden, Jacobson, & Jacobson, 2005) and ADHD (e.g., Mariani & Barkley, 1997). For this reason, it is quite likely that their performance on the Arithmetic subtests is lower than their actual performance level. Additionally, this subtest includes only arithmetic word solving problems and therefore, the Arithmetic subtest does not accurately represent overall mathematics performance.

Academic performance of children/individuals with FASD. For younger children with FASD, the findings for academic performance were inconclusive. Goldschmidt, Richardson, Stoffer, Geva and Day (1996) examined the 512 children (M_{age} = 6.5, SD = 0.5, mean full scale IQ = 91.4) who were prenatally exposed to alcohol (mostly low to moderate exposure). In their study, children exhibited a low average range on the Arithmetic, Reading and Spelling subtests of the Wide Range Achievement Test - Revised (WRAT-R). Although lower scores were significantly correlated to the high level of alcohol exposure in the second trimester of pregnancy, scores were within the average range after controlling for IQ. The study by Jirikowic et al. (2008) reported earlier used the Academic subscale of the Social Skills Rating Scale (SSRS), Based on teacher report, children with FASD (mean full scale IQ = 91.2 on the Test of Nonverbal Intelligence) did not differ from the normal control group. However, children with FASD in this study scored significantly lower than the normal control group on spelling (mean = 86.1) and arithmetic subtests (mean = 81.2) of the WRAT3, which were both within the below average range. The result suggests that teachers tend to underestimate the mathematics problems of children with FASD.

Difficulties with academic performance for children with FASD became more significant in adolescence. Olson et al. (1998) reported that the Arithmetic scores on the WRAT-R for adolescents with FASD aged 14 to 16 years was more than 1 SD below the mean (i.e., 83.0). Although participants exhibited borderline to average IQ (mean full scale IQ = 91.1, VIQ = 87.7), there were still discrepancies between their cognitive level and the Arithmetic achievement. In contrast, reading and spelling scores were within the low average range (98.9 and 95.9, respectively) and were slightly higher than their cognitive level. The study by Howell et al. (2006) noted in the *Adaptive Functioning* section included children (54 boys and 74 girls, age range = 13 to 17) with prenatal alcohol exposure, who were divided into two groups according to the presence or absence of dysmorphia. Presence of dysmorphia often indicates more severe damage from prenatal alcohol exposure. Forty-six children with dysmorphia (M_{age}= 15.14, SD = 1.08, mean full scale IQ = 72.35) exhibited lower achievement levels in the areas of basic reading, spelling, and mathematics on the Wechsler Individual Achievement Test-Second Edition (WIAT-II), about 1.5 SD below the mean for basic reading and spelling, and 2 SD below for mathematics. The pattern was the same for the 82 children without dysmorphia (M_{age}= 14.86, SD = 0.83, mean full scale IQ = 78.37) in that they scored about 1 SD below the mean on basic reading and spelling, and 1.5 SD below the mean on mathematics. During adulthood, difficulties in academics became even more apparent. The level of reading was at fourth grade, spelling at third, and arithmetic at second grade on the WRAT3 (Streissguth et al., 1991).

With regard to difficulties in mathematics, one study examined the difficulties in further detail, and children with FASD (12 years old or older) exhibited impaired

32

performance in calculation involving addition, subtraction and multiplication, as well as in approximate subtraction, proximity judgment, and cognitive estimation (e.g., What is the height of the White House?) compared to a matched control group (Kopera-Frye, Dehaene, & Streissguth, 1996). In particular, the cognitive estimation task was one of the best measures discriminating the performance of children in the two groups. In contrast, the two groups did not differ in the areas of number reading, number dictation, and number comparison. In other words, children with FASD had the ability to read, write, and count numbers, but had difficulty with calculation and estimation. The researchers discussed that this lack of sense regarding number magnitude may lead to difficulties in subsequent acquisition of other higher-order mathematics abilities. This tendency was also reflected on adolescents' self-ratings. Olson, Streissguth, Sampson, Barr, Bookstein, and Thiede (1997) reported that adolescents with prenatal alcohol exposure reported low grades in mathematics during the school year, and they did not perceive themselves as good students.

Academic performance of children/individuals with ADHD. Children with ADHD are also known to have significant difficulties with academic performance compared to normally developing children (e.g., Frazier, Demaree, & Youngstrom, 2004). However, results of a meta-analysis of the published literature to determine the magnitude of achievement problems associated with ADHD indicated that the difficulties experienced by children with ADHD become less pronounced over time (Frazier et al., 2007), which is different from the tendency observed in children with FASD. Furthermore, the results of the meta-analysis indicated that children with ADHD exhibit the most difficulty in reading, followed by mathematics, and then spelling. The differences in difficulties among these three areas were statistically significant. Other studies also

33

indicated significant difficulties in reading and mathematics compared to the normal control group (e.g., Biederman, Faraone, Milberger, & Guite, 1996; Frazier et al., 2004).

Regarding achievement in spelling, previous findings were incongruent about whether achievement of children with ADHD was significantly lower than that of the normal controls, but the majority of studies reported that spelling was the least impaired area among the areas of reading, mathematics and spelling. DuPaul and Stoner (2003) noted that such academic underachievement may, in part, be due to low academic engagement rates. Interestingly, the academic difficulties of children with ADHD were rated higher when using teacher/parent ratings than using more objective scales such as grade point averages (DuPaul & Stoner, 2003).

As with the studies on children with FASD, comorbid disorders are one of the biggest issues in studies of children with ADHD. Common comorbid disorders are conduct disorder (CD), oppositional defiant disorder (ODD), learning disorder/disabilities (LD). After adolescence, major depression and bipolar disorder are commonly reported comorbid disorders (Barkley, 2006). LD is "a general term that refers to a heterogeneous group of disorders manifested by significant difficulties in the acquisition and use of listening, speaking, reading, writing, reasoning, or mathematical abilities" (National Joint Committee on Learning Disabilities, 1990). With low academic engagement rate due to attention problems, which is one of the characteristics of ADHD (DuPaul & Stoner, 2003), it is reasonable that children with ADHD who also have LD exhibit difficulties in reading, spelling, and/or mathematics.

In contrast, a meta-analysis by Frazier et al. (2004) that reviewed the published literature to determine the level of achievement problems associated with ADHD revealed that children with ADHD without comorbid LD did not underperform on reading when compared to their cognitive level (i.e., IQ). Results of paired samples *t* tests

34

indicated no significant difference between the weighted effect sizes of full scale IQ and the WRAT reading subtest (Frazier et al., 2004). A more recent meta-analysis by Frazier et al. (2007) that examined the magnitude of neuropsychological problems associated with ADHD found moderate to large effect size for reading achievement based on individually administered standardized tests. This result contradicts the 2004 study findings. Frazier et al. (2007) noted that the difference between the studies in the 2004 and 2007 meta-analyses may have led to the contradictory findings. The 2004 analysis excluded studies that involved ADHD children with comorbid LD. In contrast, the 2007 study included children with ADHD who also had LD as a comorbid disorder. In other words, children with ADHD may exhibit difficulties in reading only when they have LD as a comorbid disorder.

Methodological Issues in FASD Studies

Risk of a type II error. Results of many of the studies that examined the relation between prenatal alcohol exposure and characteristics of children with FASD were inconclusive. The main reasons that led to the inconclusive findings involved methodological issues (J. L. Jacobson & Jacobson, 2005). There are various confounding factors that are relevant to FASD, and the degree to which these factors were controlled for varied considerably (Linnet et al., 2003). Additionally, the Bonferroni correction, the traditional approach used for multiple comparisons, may also increase the risk of a Type II error (J. L. Jacobson & Jacobson, 2005). By dividing $p < 0.05$ by the number of comparisons to be assessed, the risk of a Type I error decreases, but the resulting criterion (e.g., $p < 0.005$ if there are 10 outcomes) may be too strict to detect subtle but important effects of teratogens on child development. J. L. Jacobson and

Jacobson suggest limiting the number of comparisons to those supported by previous studies or clinical observations to decrease the risk of a Type II error.

Problems distinguishing confounding and mediating variables. Another methodological issue is related to distinguishing confounding variables from mediating variables (J. L. Jacobson & Jacobson, 2005). Confounding variables are those that provide an alternative explanation to the causal inference between an exposure and an outcome, such as teratogen exposure and developmental outcomes. For example, cocaine exposure confounds the causal inference between prenatal alcohol exposure and mental retardation. Mediating variables are those that "help specify the process by which the exposure impacts the outcome in question" (J. L. Jacobson & Jacobson, 2005, p.397). For example, a mediating variable to consider in the association between prenatal alcohol exposure and working memory is gestational age. The effect of prenatal alcohol exposure on working memory may be greater among those of longer gestational period (S. W. Jacobson, et al., 2004). Control of mediators as confounders in statistical analyses may result in a failure to detect the effect of an exposure on outcomes (J. L. Jacobson & Jacobson, 2005). The effect that disappears due to the inclusion of mediators in the analysis is not a spurious correlation, but rather, indicates that the mediator has an impact on the effect of the exposure on the outcome. Thus, it is critical to identify confounders and mediators prior to data analysis (J. L. Jacobson & Jacobson). Additionally, multicollinearity of confounders may lead to invalid results, especially in high-risk populations (Cohen & Cohen, 1983).

Dichotomization of levels of alcohol exposure. There are additional problems in the procedure for controlling for confounders. Linnet et al. (2003) emphasize that the dichotomization of confounding variables, especially for exposure levels, may not be sensitive to detect an association between prenatal exposure and cognitive functions.

In summary, the incongruent findings of children with dual diagnosis of FASD and ADHD and children with single ADHD diagnosis may be related to the methodological issues mentioned above, and previous studies with relatively small sample sizes. Thus, there is a need to directly compare these two populations using larger samples. Particularly, participants included should be those with an explicit diagnosis of FASD (i.e., not just "prenatally exposed to alcohol") with detailed information about possible confounding variables, and the statistical analysis should include minimal comparisons to decrease a Type II error.

Study Rationale and Purpose

This literature review demonstrated several differences between children with single ADHD diagnosis and children with dual FASD and ADHD diagnosis, particularly with regard to adaptive functioning, academic performance, and behavior characteristics. Therefore, a comparison of the characteristics of these two populations may serve to facilitate early identification of FASD among ADHD population and referral for FASD diagnosis. First, the presence of severe deficits in adaptive functioning, especially in the area of socialization with the tendency to become more pronounced as children with FASD get older, is critical to consider. Second, parents and teacher ratings of children with FASD suggest salient difficulties in externalizing behavior. Third, there exists a significant discrepancy between IQ and mathematics achievement, particularly in calculation, approximation and cognitive estimation, with more difficulty evidenced in these areas in later grades. Below is a summary of the relevant findings by characteristics of children/individuals with FASD.

37

First, adaptive functioning deficit is one of the unique characteristics of children/individuals with FASD (e.g., Jirikowic et al., 2008). Children with ADHD also exhibited difficulties in adaptive functioning, and both groups are reported to present discrepancies between their cognitive level (i.e., IQ) and the level of adaptive functioning. Given the fact that participants of most FASD studies were community samples and that most ADHD studies included clinical samples, children/individuals with FASD are likely to have more severe difficulties in adaptive functioning in a general setting, such as in schools. Whaley et al. (2001) noted that impaired adaptive functioning becomes a more unique characteristic as children with FASD get older. Another area of deficit in adaptive functioning that is evident from several studies is socialization, particularly in interpersonal skills (e.g., Thomas et al., 1998; Whaley et al., 2001).

Second, both children with single ADHD diagnosis and children with dual FASD and ADHD diagnosis present many behavior problems assessed by teacher/parent rating scales (Olson et al., 1998; Chen et al., 1994). This tendency is more apparent when these children have CD or ODD (e.g., Biederman et al., 2008). For children with dual diagnosis, profile of the CBCL will remain the same in adolescence and adulthood. In contrast, for children with single ADHD diagnosis, the profile of CBCL may either increase or decrease as they age depending on the outcomes (Steinhausen et al., 2003). Additionally, similar to the findings for adaptive functioning, children with FASD reportedly have social relationship problems, particularly social skills problems (Schonfeld et al., 2006). However, the study by Jirikowic et al. (2008) reported that the only significant difference between children with FASD and the normal control group was in the Problem Behavior area. Therefore, the results related to differences in behavior characteristics between children with the single diagnosis and children with the dual diagnosis are inconclusive.

Third, academic performance is another area where both children with FASD and children with ADHD exhibit difficulties. Interestingly, this area becomes salient for children with FASD when they get older; whereas for children with ADHD, the difficulties become less pronounced as they age (see review by Frazier et al., 2007). One plausible explanation is that among all children with ADHD, at least one third or more will no longer exhibit ADHD symptoms to meet the ADHD diagnosis by early adulthood (Barkley, Fischer, Smallish, & Fletcher, 2002).

Achievement differences between children with single ADHD diagnosis and those with dual FASD and ADHD diagnosis were reported in specific academic content areas. Children with FASD consistently exhibited difficulties in mathematics, and there were significant discrepancies between their IQ and mathematics achievement (Olson et al., 1998). Specifically, Kopera-Frye et al. (1996) found that children with FASD had difficulty particularly in calculation, approximation and cognitive estimation, which possibly leads to difficulties in higher-order mathematics activities at later grades. In contrast, children with ADHD present most significant difficulties in reading. Frazier et al. (2007) noted that this may be due to learning disabilities as a comorbid disorder because studies that excluded the participants with comorbid disorders revealed no significant difference between IQ and reading achievement (Frazier et al., 2004). It is unclear why children with FASD present more difficulties in mathematics than reading even though the majority of them also have ADHD, but it can be one of the clues for early identification of those children. Therefore, the purpose of the present study was to examine whether there are differences in adaptive functioning, behavioral characteristics, and academic performance between children with dual FASD and ADHD diagnosis (i.e., the dual diagnosis group) and children with single ADHD diagnosis (i.e., the single diagnosis group).

Chapter 3

Methods

Participants

The study was conducted through a review of existing medical records to determine whether there are differences in adaptive functioning, behavioral characteristics, and academic performance between children with dual FASD and ADHD diagnosis (i.e., the dual diagnosis group) and children with single ADHD diagnosis. The target population for this study included those with formal medical diagnosis of FASD and/or ADHD. The sample size for the study was determined using the proc power of the Statistical Analysis Software (SAS). Specifying the total number of predictors in the full model (nfullpredictors) of 5, the number of test predictors (ntestpredictors) of 1, R^2 for the full model (rsquarefull) of 0.20, the difference in R^2 (rsquarediff) of .03, and a power of .80 yielded a required sample size of 300 (150 in each of the two groups). The specified numbers were based on previous studies on behavioral characteristics (Greenbaum et al., 2009), and the power of .80 was determined to be adequate based on the recommendation by Murphy and Myors (2004). The sample for the present study included a total of 338 participants (149 individuals with single ADHD diagnosis and 189 individuals with dual diagnosis of FASD and ADHD). Assessment data for the participants were extracted from the 2006 to 2010 records from the Pediatric Specialty Clinic at the University of Minnesota.

Inclusion criteria required that these individuals were 8 to 14 years old, and had comorbid disorders common to both FASD and ADHD, including disruptive behavior disorders (e.g., oppositional defiant disorder, conduct disorder), learning disorders, anxiety disorders, and mood disorders. The mean age of participants in the present

40

study was 11.25 years (*SD* = 2.12years). Disorders/conditions known to be correlated with adaptive functioning and academic achievement such as pervasive developmental disorders (e.g., autism), genetic diseases, seizure disorder, or IQs less than 79 (i.e., cognitive disabilities) were excluded from the sample. In particular, those with cognitive disabilities were excluded, because it was assumed that they would receive special education services based on their cognitive deficits regardless of the presence of FASD. Information on the presence and level of prenatal exposure to alcohol and chemicals, age, gender, race/ethnicity, full-scale IQ scores and Index scores on the WISC-IV, socioeconomic status (based on maternal educational level; more than 12 years of education or less than 12 years), comorbid disorders, and the number of foster or adoptive placements (no placement, one to three placements, more than three placements) were collected for the sample. Tables 3.1 and 3.2 provide participant demographic information and scores on Cognitive Functioning by group, respectively. In addition, data on adaptive, behavioral, and academic functioning (described in the next section) were collected.

Measures

The assessments included (1) the Scales of Independent Behavior-Revised (SIB-R) for adaptive functioning, (2) the Achenbach Child Behavior Check List (CBCL) and the Achenbach Teacher Rating Form (TRF) for behavioral characteristics, and (3) the Woodcock Johnson Tests of Achievement- Third Edition (WJ III ACH) for academic performance.

Scales of Independent Behavior - Revised (SIB-R). The Scales of Independent Behavior - Revised (SIB-R) comprise the following clusters: Motor Skills, Social Interaction and Communication Skills, Personal Living Skills, and Community

41

Table 3.1
Summary of Demographic Information

Variable	ADHD only			FASD + ADHD			$t(336)$	χ^2
	n	%	M (SD)	n	%	M (SD)		
Age (in years)	149		10.80 (2.02)	189		11.60 (2.14)	-3.47***	
IQ	149		97.28 (12.31)	189		92.29 (8.78)	4.18***	
Gender								1.49
Male	112	75.17		130	68.78			(N = 337)
Female	37	24.83		58	30.69			
Unknown				1	0.53			
Race/Ethnicity								48.24***
Native American/Alaska Native	0	0.00		12	6.35			(N = 338)
Black	13	8.72		36	19.05			
Hispanic	1	0.67		5	2.65			
Asian/Pacific Islander	2	1.34		3	1.59			
White	85	57.05		87	46.03			
Biracial/Multiracial	10	6.71		34	17.99			
Socioeconomic Status								54.65***
High school, GED	46	31.29		4	2.15			(N= 333)
12+ years of ed.	101	68.71		182	97.85			
Number of Out-of-Home Placements								232.54***
None	140	94.00		19	10.05			(N= 331)
1 to 3	5	3.36		119	62.96			
More than 4	3	2.01		45	23.81			
Unknown	1	0.70		6	3.17			

Note. M = mean; SD = standard deviation; ADHD = attention/deficit hyperactivity disorder; FASD = fetal alcohol spectrum disorder.
$p < .05^*$, $p < .01^{**}$, $p < .001^{***}$

Table 3.2

Cognitive Functioning by Group

Variable	ADHD only			FASD + ADHD			
	n	M	SD	n	M	SD	t
Full Scale IQ	149	97.28	12.31	189	92.29	8.78	4.18***
Verbal Comprehension Index (VCI)	139	97.42	12.11	176	92.27	10.10	4.02***
Perceptual Reasoning Index (PRI)	139	102.60	13.10	175	98.66	10.47	2.89**
Working Memory Index (WMI)	143	91.48	18.01	175	92.41	11.89	-0.55
Processing Speed Index (PSI)	144	89.26	20.66	174	90.53	12.46	-0.68
Discrepancy between VCI and PRI	139	11.47	8.33	175	11.38	8.89	0.09

Note. M = mean; *SD* = standard deviation; ADHD = attention/deficit hyperactivity disorder; FASD = fetal alcohol spectrum disorder.

$p < .01$**, $p < .001$*

Living Skills (Bruininks, Woodcock, Weatherman, & Hill, 1996). The total scores for each

cluster can be converted to a Broad Independence cluster score. Each cluster includes

two to five subscales, and each subscale has approximately 20 items that are rated

using a 4-point scoring procedure (i.e., 0 for "never or rarely" to 4 for "always or almost

always does very well"). The SIB-R also includes a Maladaptive Behavior index (i.e.,

Internalized, Asocial, Externalized, and General). The manual reports reliability

measures such as internal consistency, test-retest reliability, and interrater reliability to

be over 0.90, which is strong. Validity measures, such as criterion validity and construct

validity, are also reported to be satisfactory.

Based on previous reports on the adaptive functioning of children with FASD

and children with ADHD, this study used only clusters that measured socialization,

particularly interpersonal skills (i.e., Social Interaction and Communication Skills and

Community Living Skills) to reduce the number of comparisons and minimize a Type II

error.

Child Behavior Checklist (CBCL) and Teacher Report Form (TRF). The Child

Behavior Checklist (CBCL) is a standardized rating scale used to assess behavioral and

emotional problems (Achenbach & Rescorla, 2001). It consists of 118 items that are

rated according to three levels (i.e., not true, somewhat or sometimes true, very or often

true) and 20 open-ended items about the child's daily life (e.g., hobbies, chores,

strengths, weaknesses). The CBCL is a parent rating scale; the parallel teacher rating

scale is called the Teacher Report Form (TRF) (Achenbach, 1991). Both of these forms

include the following components: Externalizing Problems (i.e., Aggressive Behavior and

Rule-Breaking Behavior), Internalizing Problems (i.e., Anxious/Depressed,

Withdrawn/Depressed, and Somatic Complaints), and Other Problems (i.e., Social

44

Problems, Thought Problems, and Attention Problems). Both forms can be either self-administered or administered by an interviewer. Reliability measures, such as test-retest reliability and interrater reliability, are reported in the manual to be around the middle to upper .90s, which is strong. However, mother's and father's ratings about their clinically-referred child are discrepant (Achenbach & Rescorla, 2001). Validity measures, such as criterion validity and construct validity, are reported to be satisfactory.

Based on previous reports on the behavioral characteristics of children with FASD and children with ADHD, this study used items related to internalizing and externalizing problems for both the CBCL and the TRF.

Woodcock Johnson Tests of Achievement- Third Edition (WJ III ACH).
Woodcock Johnson Tests of Achievement- Third Edition (WJ III ACH) is a standardized, norm-referenced achievement test that includes both the Standard and Extended batteries (Woodcock, McGrew, & Mather, 2001). The Standard battery consists of 12 subtests that measure skills in core academic areas - reading, writing and mathematics. Two of the12 subtests measure memory skills. The Extended battery consists of 10 subtests that measure additional skills (e.g., vocabulary) or in other content areas (e.g., social studies). Reliability indices reported in the manual are range from 0.80s to 0.90s for each subtest, and in the .90s for cluster scores, which is strong. Validity measures, such as criterion validity and construct validity, are also reported as satisfactory.

In this study, 10 subtests that measure core academic areas from the Standard Battery were used. Of the 12 subtests in the Standard Battery, the two subtests that measure memory skills were excluded. Based on previous reports on academic performance of children with FASD and children with ADHD, the composites that measure overall reading and math (Broad Reading and Broad Math) and the subtests in Math (Calculation, Applied Problems, and Math Fluency) were used in this study.

Study Procedures

After obtaining approval from the Institutional Review Board (IRB) at the University of Minnesota, data were collected by the author from the Pediatric Specialty Clinic at the University of Minnesota. The medical record of each participant was assigned randomly an ID number, and the list of ID numbers that were matched to medical record numbers was saved as a different document with a password protection. Therefore, each hard-copy data sheet only included the assigned ID number, demographic information, and the test scores retrieved manually from the medical record database. The electronic datasets generated based on the hard-copy data sheets were password-protected and stored in a computer that was not connected to any network. To examine the reliability of the data collection, the author generated 10 percent of the hard-copy data twice. That is, data were retrieved twice from the medical record database at different times. The reliability coefficient for this data was satisfactory (r = .97). Moreover, the electronic datasets were entered twice separately and matched to each other to ensure the accuracy of data entry.

Data Analysis

An analysis of covariance (ANCOVA) was used to determine whether there are differences in adaptive functioning, behavioral characteristics, and academic performance between children with dual FASD and ADHD diagnosis (i.e., the dual diagnosis group) and children with single ADHD diagnosis. ANCOVA was selected because it can be used to examine the effects of categorical variables (i.e., independent variables) on a continuous dependent variable while controlling for other variables (i.e.,

46

covariates) that covary with the dependent variable (Howell, 2001). In other words, ANCOVA allows to control for the variables that cannot be randomized to maximally reduce the differences between the two groups due to these variables.

The data analysis procedures consisted of first testing for the four underlying assumptions of ANCOVA followed by conducting the ANCOVA. The independent variable tested was the group (i.e., single or dual diagnosis) and the dependent variables were scores on measures of adaptive, behavioral, and academic functioning.

The four underlying assumptions of ANCOVA include normality, homogeneity of the variance (homoscedasticity), linear relation between dependent variable and covariates (linearity), and homogeneity of regression (Howell, 2010). I tested the first assumption, normality, by examining the Q-Q plots for the residuals of each dependent variable to check for the presence of potential outliers as well as used descriptive statistics (i.e., means, standard deviations, skewnesses, and kurtoses) to examine the plausibility of normality (e.g., kurtosis < 3). To test the homogeneity of the variance, the second assumption, the scatter plots of the residuals of each dependent variable and the independent variables were visually examined for similarity of the spread of the residuals. Furthermore, homogeneity of the variance was determined based on non-significant results of the Levine's test. The third assumption, the linear relation between the dependent variable and covariates was explored by examining the scatter plots of unstandardized residuals to the unstandardized predicted value of the same dependent variable. An absence of curvilinear relation was used as the basis to suggest a linear relation between the dependent variable and covariates. The fourth assumption, homogeneity of regression, was tested by examining the interaction effects for all main factors with the covariates. Homogeneity of regression assumption would be met when the interaction effects are nonsignificant. Moreover, scatter plots of dependent variables

47

and the covariates (i.e., IQ and age), as well as trends of the scatter plots for the two groups (i.e., single diagnosis and dual diagnosis) were examined visually to see if they matched.

To answer the first research question (i.e., whether there is a difference on adaptive functioning between the single and dual diagnosis groups), I fit an ANCOVA using the Social Interaction and Communication Skills scores and Community Living Skills scores in the SIB-R as the outcome variables, along with the following covariates: IQ, age, ethnicity (i.e., white or nonwhite), the number of out-of-home placements (i.e., no placement, one to two placements, three or more placements), and the presence of FASD (i.e., single or dual diagnosis). For the second research question (i.e., whether there is a difference between groups on behavior characteristics, I fit an ANCOVA using the Internalizing and Externalizing Problems scores in the CBCL and the TRF as the outcome variables, along with the following covariates: IQ, age, ethnicity, the number of out-of-home placements, and the presence of FASD. The presence of comorbid mood disorders was also included as a covariate for the Internalizing Problems scores on the CBCL and the TRF. Similarly, the presence of comorbid disruptive disorders was included as a covariate for the Externalizing Problems scores on the CBCL and the TRF. With regard to the third research question (i.e., whether there is a difference between groups on academic performance), I fit an ANCOVA using the Broad Reading composite scores, and Broad Math composite scores in the WJ-III ACH as the outcome variables, along with the following covariates: IQ, age, ethnicity, the number of out-of-home placements, the presence of comorbid LD, and the presence of FASD. In sum, ANCOVA for each dependent variable was conducted using the following independent variables/covariates: age, number of out-of-home placements, presence of comorbid mood disorders (for internalizing behavior only), disruptive disorders (for externalizing

48

behavior only) and LD (for overall reading and mathematics only), and the presence of FASD.

All the covariates were known to affect dependent variables from previous studies (see a review in *Chapter 2*) and also showed significant differences between the two groups (see Table 3.1). Regarding the number of out-of-home placements, ethnicity and SES (based on maternal educational level), previous studies reported high overlap among the three variables (e.g., Hill, 2005; Hansen et al., 2004). Results of spearman correlations examining the relationships among the three variables indicated that the number of out-of-home placements and SES were significantly correlated with each other (Table 3.3). The number of out-of-home placements showed higher variance (.51) than SES. As such, the number of out-of-home placements was used for the analysis. To estimate the practice significance of the effects, effect sizes were calculated as follows: $d = [x_1 - x_2] / \sqrt{MS_{error}})$. That is, the mean difference between the adjusted scores of the two groups was divided by the square root of the mean square error from an analysis of variance as an estimate of the average variability within each group (Howell, 2010).

The Bonferroni correction is a method to decrease Type I error (i.e., false positives) for multiple comparisons by maintaining the family-wise error rate (Dunn, 1961). That is, dividing a statistical significance level (usually $p < .05$) by the number of dependent variables. However, this method is often criticized for not controlling for Type II error (i.e., false negatives). That is, when the number of dependent variables is large, a statistical significance level can be too small to detect a subtle but important effect due to reduced power (e.g., Perneger, 1998; Jacobson & Jacobson, 2005). Thus, to maximally decrease Type II error, the number of comparisons was limited to eight sub-

49

domains within the three measures: the Social Interaction and Communication Skills and Community Living Skills domain in the SIB-R, the Internalizing and Externalizing Problems in both the CBCL and the TRF, and the Broad Reading composite and Broad Math composite in the WJ-III ACH. Moreover, the Holm-Bonferroni method, which is known to be less conservative (i.e., has a smaller risk of Type II error), was used (Holm, 1979). That is, the method first rank orders all the p-values, and compares the smallest p-value to α/k (k = number of comparisons; in this case, p = .05 divided by eight, p =.00625). If the first comparison is significant, the next smallest p-value is compared to $\alpha/(k\text{-}1)$, and the process is continued until p-value is not significant. All the remaining p-values below the nonsignificant p-value are considered nonsignificant.

Table 3.3
Spearman Correlation Coefficients Among Covariates

	# of Out-of-Home Placements	SES	Ethnicity
# of Out-of-Home Placements	---	.40***	-.10
SES	.40***	---	-.03
Ethnicity	-.10	-.03	---

Note. Ethnicity = white or nonwhite
*** $p < .001$

Chapter 4

Results

In this chapter, demographics of the participants and the underlying assumptions of ANCOVA are presented first, because it is critical to understand these fundamental factors that impact the findings in this study. Then, three major findings related to adaptive functioning, behavioral characteristics, and academic performance are presented.

Demographic characteristics of the Participants

Results indicated statistically significant between-group differences on IQ, SES, and the number of foster/adoptive placements (see Table 3.1 in the *Methods* section). Participants in the single diagnosis group were younger, $t(336) = 12.05$, $p < .001$, had higher SES scores, χ^2 (1, $N = 333$) 54.45, $p = .001$, and most of them lived with their families, χ^2 (2, $N = 331$) $= 232.54$, $p = .001$, compared to participants in the dual diagnosis group. With regard to cognitive functioning, those in the single diagnosis group exhibited higher full scale IQ scores, $t(336) = 18.83$, $p < .001$, higher Verbal Comprehension Index (VCI: represents the ability to process and understand verbal stimuli) scores, $t(313) = 16.89$, $p < .001$, and higher Perceptual Reasoning Index (PRI: represents the ability to process and understand visual stimuli) scores, $t(312) = 8.75$, $p < .01$. There were no significant differences between the two groups on the Working Memory Index and Processing Speed Index scores as well as a discrepancy between the VCI and the PRI scores (see Table 3.2 in the *Methods* section). Although there were more males than females in the two groups (242 and 95, respectively), there was no statistically significant difference between groups regarding male-to-female ratio. Table 4.1 presents information for the two groups by subtypes.

Table 4.1

Frequency and Percentage of ADHD and FASD Subtypes by Group

Subtype	ADHD only		FASD + ADHD		$\chi^2 (df = 4)$
	n	%	n	%	
ADHD					61.79***
Inattentive	55	36.91	23	12.17	
Hyperactive-Impulsive	1	0.67	3	1.59	
Combined	46	30.87	100	52.91	
NOS	26	17.45	5	2.65	
Unspecified	21	14.09	58	30.69	
FASD					
FAS			21	11.11	
Partial FAS			64	33.86	
ARND			98	51.85	
Unspecified			6	3.17	

Note. ADHD = attention/deficit hyperactivity disorder; FASD = fetal alcohol spectrum disorder; FAS = fetal alcohol Syndrome; NOS = not otherwise specified; ARND = alcohol related neurodevelopmental disorder.

$p < .001$***

Table 4.1 indicates that the two groups significantly differed in terms of ADHD subtypes, $\chi^2(4, N = 338) = 61.79$, $p = .001$. Approximately 30% of the participants in the single diagnosis group were the Predominantly Inattentive (PI) type, whereas only 12% of the dual diagnosis group included the PI type, and approximately half of the participants in the dual diagnosis group were identified as the Combined (C) type (see Table 4.1). The representation of Predominantly Hyperactive-Impulsive category was low for both single diagnosis (0.7%) and dual diagnosis (1.6%) groups. Regarding FASD subtypes, approximately half (52%) of the participants in the dual diagnosis group had alcohol related neurodevelopmental disorder, followed by partial FAS, and FAS (34% and 11%, respectively).

Next, the groups were compared on comorbid disorders. The results of the comparisons between the two groups are presented in Table 4.2. Approximately 40% in the single diagnosis group and 35% in the dual diagnosis group had no other comorbid disorders (Table 4.2). Learning disorders (LD), disruptive disorders, and mood disorders were the three major comorbid disorders in the single ADHD diagnosis group (19%, 21%, and 19%, respectively), whereas disruptive disorder was the major comorbid disorder in the dual diagnosis group (40%). Additionally, there were significant differences between the two groups regarding comorbid learning disorders, $\chi^2 (1, N = 338) = 8.73$, $p = .003$, disruptive behavior disorders, $\chi^2 (1, N = 338) = 12.33$, $p = .001$, mood disorders, $\chi^2 (1, N = 338) = 6.88$, $p = .009$, and other disorders, $\chi^2 (1, N = 338) = 4.75$, $p = .029$.

Table 4.2
Frequency and Percentage of Comorbid disorders by Group

	ADHD only		FASD + ADHD		
	n	%	*n*	%	χ^2 (*df* = 1)
No Comorbid Disorder	60	40.27	67	35.45	
Learning Disorders	29	19.46	16	8.47	8.731**
Disruptive Disorders	32	21.48	74	39.15	12.332***
Mood Disorders	29	19.46	18	9.52	6.875**
Anxiety Disorders	17	11.41	24	12.70	0.13
Other	22	14.77	46	24.34	4.752*

Note. Some participants exhibited more than one disorder, therefore total percentage exceeds 100%.
ADHD = attention/deficit hyperactivity disorder; FASD = fetal alcohol spectrum disorder.
p < .05*, *p* < .01**, *p* < .001***

It is important to note that the two groups differed with regard to the presence of prenatal exposure to teratogens (Table 4.3). As described earlier, only one participant was prenatally exposed to chemicals (details unknown) in the single diagnosis group. In contrast, only two participants in the dual diagnosis group were not exposed to chemicals. About half of the participants (49.5%) were exposed to chemicals, and the other half (49.5%) was possibly exposed to chemicals (including those who were highly likely to be exposed to chemicals, but missing a confirmation by a reliable source). The difference between the two groups regarding chemical exposure was statistically significant, χ^2 (3, N = 338) = 326.00, p = .001.

Underlying Assumptions for ANCOVA

Before interpreting the results of ANCOVA, the underlying assumptions were tested: normality, homogeneity of the variance (homoscedasticity), linear relation between dependent variable and covariates (linearity), and homogeneity of regression. For the first assumption of normality, the Q-Q plots (See Figure 4.1- 4.8 in *Appendix* section) showed that there were several potential outliers for several dependent variables. The main analyses were conducted with and without these outliers to reveal the impact on the results of the analyses, and, as a result, one to four potential outliers in the Social Interaction and Communication domain and the Community Living domain of the SIB-R and the Broad Reading composite of the WJ-III ACH were excluded. Afterward, descriptive statistics of each dependent variable indicated that the normality of the variables was not seriously violated (Table 4.4).

Table 4.3

Presence and Level of Exposure to Teratogens by Group

	ADHD only		FASD + ADHD		
	n	%	n	%	$\chi^2\,(df = 3)$
Alcohol					338.00***
No Exposure	149	100.00	0	0.00	
Yes- Mild	0	0.00	14	7.41	
Yes- Details Unknown	0	0.00	80	42.33	
Yes- Extensive	0	0.00	70	37.04	
[†]Exposure Unknown	0	0.00	25	13.23	
Chemicals					326.00***
No Exposure	148	99.33	2	1.06	
Exposure Unknown (includes [††]exposure suspected)	0	0.00	93	49.21	
Yes- Details Unknown	1	0.67	68	35.98	
Yes- Extensive	0	0.00	26	13.76	

Note. ADHD = attention/deficit hyperactivity disorder; FASD = fetal alcohol spectrum disorder.

[†]Exposure unknown = all the children had FAS (showed facial features unique to alcohol exposure present)

[††]Exposure suspected = chemical exposure was highly suspected, but no confirmation was available.

$p < .001$***

Table 4.4

Descriptive Statistics for the Dependent Variables

Measure	N	Minimum	Maximum	Mean	SD	Skewness	Kurtosis
SIB-R							
Social Interaction & Communication	212	27	133	82.47	20.00	.08	-.19
Community Living	209	21	129	74.09	20.80	-.03	-.42
CBCL							
Internalizing Behavior	312	33	91	63.23	9.92	-.44	.09
Externalizing Behavior	312	33	94	67.08	11.85	-.70	.18
TRF							
Internalizing Behavior	203	37	86	58.34	10.25	-.33	-.37
Externalizing Behavior	203	41	85	61.48	10.63	-.06	-.38
WJ-III ACH							
Broad Reading	283	58	135	93.40	12.58	.02	.84
Broad Math	290	64	128	94.57	11.61	.13	.08

Note. Higher scores on the CBCL/TRF indicate more severe behavior. SIB-R = Scales of Independent Behavior-Revised; CBCL = Achenbach Child Behavior Checklist; TRF = Achenbach Teacher Report Form; WJ-III ACH = Woodcock Johnson Tests of Achievement- Third Edition.

For instance, kurtosis statistics of the variables were less than three, which indicated that the normality of all the variables was satisfied. For the second assumption of homoscedasticity, scatter plots of the residuals for each dependent variable against the independent variables indicated that the spread of the residuals of each dependent variable appeared similar across the independent variables (See Figure 4.9- 4.32 in *Appendix*). Additionally, the Levine's test was nonsignificant for all the dependent variables, with the exception of Internalizing and externalizing behaviors of the CBCL. For these two dependent variables, the ratio of the standard deviation of the two groups (i.e., the single diagnosis group and the dual diagnosis group) was less than 4:1 (i.e., 1.53 and 1.14 for the internalizing behavior, and 1.55 and 0.97 for the externalizing behavior), indicating that the underlying assumption of the homogeneity of the variance was not seriously violated. For the third assumption of linearity, the scatter plots of unstandardized residuals of each dependent variable and unstandardized predicted value of the same dependent variable indicated no curvilinear relations, suggesting that linearity assumption was satisfied (see Figure 4.33- 4.40 in *Appendix*). For the fourth assumption of homogeneity of regressions, there were no interaction effects for all main effects with the covariates for all the dependent variables, with the exception of the number of out-of-home placements by white for the Internalizing Behavior of the CBCL and the Broad Math of the WJ-III ACH, as well as the number of out-of-home placements by age for the Externalizing Behavior of the CBCL, indicating that this assumption was almost met (Table 4.5). Additionally, there were no serious mismatches in trends of the scatter plots of the two groups, indicating that homogeneity of regression was satisfied (see Figures 4.41- 4.56 in the *Appendix*). In sum, with all the four underlying assumption satisfied, the interpretations of the result of ANCOVA were valid.

Table 4.5

ANOVA table for the interaction of all main effects with the covariates on Social Interaction and Communication of the SIB-R

Source	Type III Sum of Squares	df	Mean Square	F	p
Corrected Model	14930.46	20	746.52	1.78*	.03
Intercept	357.67	1	357.67	0.85	.36
White	160.34	1	160.34	0.38	.54
Placements	183.17	2	91.59	0.22	.80
FASD	96.86	1	96.86	0.23	.63
Age	166.8	1	166.86	0.40	.53
WISC_FSIQ	39.90	1	39.90	0.10	.76
White * Placements	261.18	2	130.59	0.31	.73
White * FASD	74.74	1	74.74	0.18	.67
White * Age	3.16	1	3.16	0.01	.93
White * WISC_FSIQ	265.67	1	265.67	0.63	.43
Placements * FASD	1570.69	2	785.34	1.87	.16
Placements * Age	213.54	2	106.77	0.25	.78
Placements * WISC_FSIQ	12.19	2	6.09	0.02	.99
FASD * Age	39.22	1	39.22	0.09	.76
FASD * WISC_FSIQ	151.76	1	151.76	0.36	.55
Age * WISC_FSIQ	121.82	1	121.82	0.29	.59
Error	79831.58	190	420.17		
Total	1536083.00	211			
Corrected Total	94762.05	210			

Note. SIB-R = Scales of Independent Behavior-Revised; FASD = fetal alcohol spectrum disorder (not FASD = 0, FASD = 1); Placements = out-of-home placements; FSIQ = full scale IQ.
$p < .05$*

Potential Indicators for Identifying Children with Dual FASD and ADHD Diagnosis Group

As mentioned in the *Methods* section, the Holm-Bonferroni method was used to control Type I error (Holm, 1979). There were eight comparisons in the present study, and all the p-values for the covariates, the presence of FASD (i.e., FASD or not), were rank-ordered (Table 4.6). As a result, only the first two comparisons were significant, and the rest of the comparisons were nonsignificant. Additionally, significance levels of the other covariates were determined based on the same α level for the presence of FASD. For those where the presence of FASD was nonsignificant, $p < .00625$ (i.e., .05 divided by eight) was used.

Adaptive functioning. Adaptive functioning was measured using scores on the Scales of Independent Behavior-Revised (SIB-R). Of the four clusters, only the Social Interaction and Communication Skills and Community Living Skills clusters were analyzed to reduce the number of comparisons (Table 4.7). There was no statistically significant effect of the presence of FASD on the Social Interaction and Communication Skills, $F(1, 201) = 0.04$, $p = .85$ (Table 4.8), or on the Community Living Skills, $F(1, 198) = 3.85$, $p = .05$ (Table 4.9). However, IQ was significantly related to both the Social Interaction and Communication Skills, $F(1, 201) = 16.79$, $p < .001$, and the Community Living Skills, $F(1, 198) = 18.68$, $p < .001$, with higher IQ scores related to higher adaptive functioning scores.

Behavioral Characteristics. Behavioral characteristics were assessed using the Internalizing Problems' and Externalizing Problems' scores on the Achenbach Child Behavior Check List (CBCL) and the Achenbach Teacher Rating Form (TRF). Overall, parents rated their children's problems significantly higher (i.e., more severe) than

Table 4.6

P-values for the "Presence of FASD" from all the ANOVA Tables based on the Holm-Bonferroni Method

Order	Measure	p	α	Adjusted α	Significance
1	CBCL: Externalizing Behavior	.001	.05	.00625	Significant
2	TRF: Externalizing Behavior	.001	.05	.00714	Significant
3	SIB-R: Community Living	.051	.05	.008	Not significant
4	WJ-III ACH: Broad Reading	.132	.05	---	Not significant
5	WJ-III ACH: Broad Math	.205	.05	---	Not significant
6	TRF: Internalizing Behavior	.265	.05	---	Not significant
7	CBCL: Internalizing Behavior	.590	.05	---	Not significant
8	SIB-R: Social Interaction & Communication	.848	.05	---	Not significant

Note. FASD = fetal alcohol spectrum disorder; SIB-R = Scales of Independent Behavior-Revised; CBCL = Achenbach Child Behavior Checklist; TRF = Achenbach Teacher Report Form; WJ-III ACH = Woodcock Johnson Tests of Achievement- Third Edition;

Table 4.7

Means and Standard Deviations for Adaptive Functioning, Behavioral Characteristics, and Achievement Measures by Group

Measure	ADHD only (single)			FASD + ADHD (dual)			
	n	*M*	*SD*	*n*	*M*	*SD*	ES
SIB-R							
Social Interaction & Communication	37	88.19	18.92	175	81.26	20.01	
Adjusted Social Interaction & Communication		(82.84)			(81.91)		0.05
Community Living	36	82.36	17.46	173	72.36	21.07	
Adjusted Community Living		(81.89)			(71.58)		0.52
CBCL							
Internalizing Behavior	141	61.79	10.20	171	64.42	9.54	
Adjusted Internalizing Behavior		(65.51)			(66.60)		-0.11
Externalizing Behavior	141	61.79	12.36	171	71.44	9.43	
Adjusted Externalizing Behavior		(65.24)			(72.20)		-0.70
TRF							
Internalizing Behavior	87	57.78	10.02	116	58.76	10.45	
Adjusted Internalizing Behavior		(59.09)			(61.84)		-0.28
Externalizing Behavior	87	57.79	10.42	116	64.24	9.95	
Adjusted Externalizing Behavior		(58.90)			(66.38)		-0.79
WJ-III ACH							
Broad Reading	115	94.85	11.86	168	92.40	12.99	
Adjusted Broad Reading		(91.14)			(87.81)		0.33
Broad Math	117	97.16	10.78	173	92.82	11.86	
Adjusted Broad Math		(94.10)			(91.73)		0.27

Note. Numbers in each cell are raw scores and the numbers in parentheses are adjusted scores; higher scores on the CBCL/TRF indicate more severe behavior. ADHD = attention/deficit hyperactivity disorder; FASD = fetal alcohol spectrum disorder; SIB-R = Scales of Independent Behavior-Revised; CBCL = Achenbach Child Behavior Checklist; TRF = Achenbach Teacher Report Form; WJ-III ACH = Woodcock Johnson Tests of Achievement- Third Edition; ES = Effect size (Cohen's *d*)

Table 4.8

ANOVA table for the Social Interaction and Communication of the SIB-R

Source	Type III Sum of Squares	df	Mean Square	F	p	Partial Eta Squared
Corrected Model	11886.10	6	1981.02	5.62	.000	.14
Intercept	2097.18	1	2097.18	5.95	.016	.03
FASD or not	12.94	1	12.94	0.04	.848	.00
White or Nonwhite	1160.44	1	1160.44	3.29	.071	.02
# of Placements	2211.54	2	1105.77	3.14	.045	.03
FSIQ	5917.11	1	5917.11	16.79	.000	.08
Age	391.35	1	391.35	1.11	.293	.01
Error	70817.73	201	352.33			
Total	1490824.00	208				
Corrected Total	82703.83	207				

Note. SIB-R = Scales of Independent Behavior-Revised; FASD = fetal alcohol spectrum disorder (not FASD = 0, FASD = 1); Placements = out-of-home placements; FSIQ = full scale IQ.

Table 4.9

ANOVA table for the Community Living of the SIB-R

Source	Type III Sum of Squares	df	Mean Square	F	p	Partial Eta Squared
Corrected Model	11187.90	6	1864.65	4.72	.000	.13
Intercept	502.70	1	502.70	1.27	.260	.01
FASD or not	1521.36	1	1521.36	3.85	.051	.02
White or Nonwhite	252.33	1	252.33	0.64	.425	.00
# of Placements	244.81	2	122.41	0.31	.734	.00
FSIQ	7374.88	1	7374.88	18.68	.000	.09
Age	14.66	1	14.66	0.04	.847	.00
Error	78153.14	198	394.71			
Total	1209850.00	205				
Corrected Total	89341.04	204				

Note. SIB-R = Scales of Independent Behavior-Revised; FASD = fetal alcohol spectrum disorder (not FASD = 0, FASD = 1); Placements = out-of-home placements; FSIQ = full scale IQ.

teachers on both the Internalizing Problems, $t(201) = 4.99$, $p < .001$, and Externalizing Problems, $t(201) = 7.06$, $p < .001$. The presence of FASD was not significantly related to the internalizing behavior on both the CBCL, $F(1, 299) = 0.29$, $p = .59$ (Table 4.10), and the TRF, $F(1, 192) = 1.25$, $p = .27$ (Table. 4.12). However, the presence of comorbid mood disorders was significantly related to internalizing behavior on the CBCL, $F(1, 299) = 17.93$, $p < .001$, with the presence of mood disorders related to higher scores (i.e., more severe internalizing behavior), but not the TRF, $F(1, 192) = 6.11$, $p = .01$. In contrast, the presence of FASD was significantly related to externalizing behavior on both the CBCL, $F(1, 299) = 10.96$, $p < .001$ (Table 4.11), and the TRF, $F(192) = 10.43$, $p < .001$ (Table 4.13), with the presence of FASD related to higher scores (i.e., more severe externalizing behavior). In particular, the presence of FASD showed large effect sizes of -0.70 on the CBCL and -0.79 on the TRF. Additionally, the presence of comorbid disruptive disorders significantly related to more externalizing behavior on the CBCL, $F(1, 299) = 51.76$, $p < .001$, and on the TRF, $F(1, 192) = 26.20$, $p < .001$.

Academic Performance. Academic performance was measured using scores on the WJ III ACH. In this study, the composite scores for reading and mathematics (Broad Reading and Broad Math) were analyzed. Independent variables/covariates used for ANCOVA were the presence of FASD, IQ, age, ethnicity (i.e., white or nonwhite), number of out-of-home placements, and comorbid LD. The presence of FASD was not significantly related to broad reading, $F(1, 268) = 2.28$, $p = .13$ (Table 4.14), nor broad mathematics, $F(1, 275) = 1.62$, $p = .21$ (Table. 4.15). In contrast, the presence of comorbid LD was significantly related to both lower overall reading achievement, $F(1, 268) = 41.87$, $p < .001$, and lower overall mathematics achievement, $F(1, 275) = 18.85$, $p < .001$. Furthermore, higher IQ was significantly related to higher overall reading achievement, $F(1, 268) = 102.78$, $p < .001$, and to higher overall mathematics achievement, $F(1, 275) = 0.50$, $p < .001$. Also, older age was significantly related

Table 4.10

ANOVA table for the Internalizing Behavior of the CBCL

Source	Type III Sum of Squares	df	Mean Square	F	p	Partial Eta Squared
Corrected Model	2569.02	7	367.00	4.03	.000	.09
Intercept	11782.71	1	11782.71	129.23	.000	.30
FASD or not	26.56	1	26.56	0.29	.590	.00
White or Nonwhite	35.75	1	35.75	0.39	.532	.00
# of Placements	223.89	2	111.95	1.23	.294	.01
FSIQ	46.02	1	46.02	0.51	.478	.00
Age	5.13	1	5.13	0.06	.813	.00
Comorbid Mood Disorder	1634.91	1	1634.91	17.93	.000	.06
Error	27262.55	299	91.18			
Total	1250962.00	307				
Corrected Total	29831.56	306				

Note. CBCL = Achenbach Child Behavior Checklist; FASD = fetal alcohol spectrum disorder (not FASD = 0, FASD = 1); Placements = out-of-home placements; FSIQ = full scale IQ.

Table 4.11

ANOVA table for the Externalizing Behavior of the CBCL

Source	Type III Sum of Squares	df	Mean Square	F	p	Partial Eta Squared
Corrected Model	13528.57	7	1932.65	19.35	.000	.31
Intercept	16861.93	1	16861.93	168.85	.000	.36
FASD or not	1094.64	1	1094.64	10.96	.001	.04
White or Nonwhite	88.12	1	88.12	0.88	.348	.00
# of Placements	47.83	2	23.92	0.24	.787	.00
FSIQ	552.66	1	552.66	5.53	.019	.02
Age	7.31	1	7.31	0.07	.787	.00
Comorbid DBD	5168.95	1	5168.95	51.76	.000	.15
Error	29859.69	299	99.87			
Total	1425400.00	307				
Corrected Total	43388.26	306				

Note. CBCL = Achenbach Child Behavior Checklist; FASD = fetal alcohol spectrum disorder (not FASD = 0, FASD = 1); DBD = disruptive behavior disorders; Placements = out-of-home placements; FSIQ = full scale IQ.

Table 4.12

ANOVA table for the Internalizing Behavior of the TRF

Source	Type III Sum of Squares	df	Mean Square	F	p	Partial Eta Squared
Corrected Model	1771.26	7	253.04	2.57	.015	.09
Intercept	7687.31	1	7687.31	78.13	.000	.29
FASD or not	123.02	1	123.02	1.25	.265	.01
White or Nonwhite	169.72	1	169.72	1.73	.191	.01
# of Placements	500.62	2	250.31	2.54	.081	.03
FSIQ	336.70	1	336.70	3.42	.066	.02
Age	4.36	1	4.36	0.04	.833	.00
Comorbid Mood Disorder	601.02	1	601.02	6.11	.014	.03
Error	18890.62	192	98.39			
Total	704527.00	200				
Corrected Total	20661.88	199				

Note. TRF = Achenbach Teacher Report Form; FASD = fetal alcohol spectrum disorder (not FASD = 0, FASD = 1); Placements = out-of-home placements; FSIQ = full scale IQ.

Table 4.13

ANOVA table for the Externalizing Behavior of the TRF

Source	Type III Sum of Squares	df	Mean Square	F	p	Partial Eta Squared
Corrected Model	5580.86	7	797.27	8.96	.000	.25
Intercept	8711.18	1	8711.18	97.90	.000	.34
FASD or not	927.84	1	927.84	10.43	.001	.05
White or Nonwhite	262.69	1	262.69	2.95	.087	.02
# of Placements	397.29	2	198.64	2.23	.110	.02
FSIQ	155.43	1	155.43	1.75	.188	.01
Age	47.84	1	47.84	0.54	.464	.00
Comorbid DBD	2331.07	1	2331.07	26.20	.000	.12
Error	17084.97	192	88.98			
Total	779854.00	200				
Corrected Total	22665.82	199				

Note. TRF = Achenbach Teacher Report Form; FASD = fetal alcohol spectrum disorder (not FASD = 0, FASD = 1); DBD = disruptive behavior disorders; Placements = out-of-home placements; FSIQ = full scale IQ.

Table 4.14

ANOVA table for Broad Reading of the WJ-III ACH

Source	Type III Sum of Squares	df	Mean Square	F	p	Partial Eta Squared
Corrected Model	16012.35	7	2287.48	21.85	.000	.36
Intercept	1220.05	1	1220.05	11.66	.001	.04
FASD or not	238.77	1	238.77	2.28	.132	.01
White or Nonwhite	62.32	1	62.32	0.60	.441	.00
# of Placements	142.80	2	71.40	0.68	.506	.01
FSIQ	10757.91	1	10757.91	102.78	.000	.28
Age	51.78	1	51.78	0.50	.482	.00
Comorbid LD	4382.84	1	4382.84	41.87	.000	.14
Error	28052.04	268	104.67			
Total	2445905.00	276				
Corrected Total	44064.39	275				

Note. WJ-III ACH = Woodcock Johnson Tests of Achievement- Third Edition; FASD = fetal alcohol spectrum disorder (not FASD = 0, FASD = 1); Placements = out-of-home placements; FSIQ = full scale IQ; LD = learning disorders.

Table 4.15

ANOVA table for Broad Math of the WJ-III ACH

Source	Type III Sum of Squares	df	Mean Square	F	p	Partial Eta Squared
Corrected Model	15811.14	7	2258.74	29.42	.000	.43
Intercept	5185.19	1	5185.19	67.53	.000	.20
FASD or not	124.12	1	124.12	1.62	.205	.01
White or Nonwhite	21.09	1	21.09	0.28	.601	.00
# of Placements	401.44	2	200.72	2.61	.075	.02
FSIQ	9627.73	1	9627.73	125.39	.000	.31
Age	2321.73	1	2321.73	30.24	.000	.10
Comorbid LD	1447.18	1	1447.18	18.85	.000	.06
Error	21114.86	275	76.78			
Total	2561447.00	283				
Corrected Total	36926.01	282				

Note. WJ-III ACH = Woodcock Johnson Tests of Achievement- Third Edition; FASD = fetal alcohol spectrum disorder (not FASD = 0, FASD = 1); Placements = out-of-home placements; FSIQ = full scale IQ; LD = learning disorders.

to lower overall mathematics achievement, $F(1, 275) = 30.24$, $p < .001$, but not to overall

reading achievement, $F(1, 268) = 0.50$, $p = .48$.

Chapter 5

Discussion

In this chapter, demographic characteristics of the two groups are discussed first because these differences appeared to affect the findings to some extent. Then, each of the study findings is discussed, and, lastly, the limitations of the present study and implications for future studies are described.

Demographic characteristics of the Participants

Results revealed that participants with single ADHD diagnosis, namely those with ADHD who were not exposed to alcohol, had more protective factors (i.e., higher IQ and SES) and fewer risk factors (i.e., not experiencing out-of-home placements) than those with dual diagnosis. These differences in risk/protective factors between the two groups support the findings of previous research by Greenbaum et al. (2009) that also compared children with ADHD and children with FASD (including both children with the dual ADHD and FASD diagnosis as well as those with single FASD diagnosis). Most of the participants in the single diagnosis group in the present study were not prenatally exposed to other teratogens (e.g., cocaine, marijuana, nicotine), whereas many of those in the dual diagnosis group were exposed to chemicals, including cocaine, nicotine and other drugs. This is expected given that the use of chemicals among individuals who exhibit alcohol use disorders is higher than that in the general public (Stinson et al., 2005). Furthermore, research suggests that those who exhibit both alcohol and drug use disorders are more likely to have lower SES (i.e., income) and less education (Stinson et al., 2005), which characterizes the dual diagnosis group in the present study. Because of

70

the lack of overlap regarding exposure to chemicals between the two groups, the chemical exposure could not be controlled.

With regard to the rate of comorbid disorders, learning disorders and mood disorders that characterize the two major comorbid disorders of ADHD (e.g., American Academy of Pediatrics, 2000) were each observed in approximately 20% of the single diagnosis group. In contrast, the percentages of these disorders were half as likely to be observed (8.5% and 9.5%, respectively) in the dual diagnosis group, and the difference between the two groups with regard to both comorbid disorders were statistically significant. The other major comorbid disorder of ADHD, disruptive behavior disorders, was observed nearly twice as much (39.2%) in the dual diagnosis group than in the single diagnosis group (21.5%), which was also significantly different between the two groups.

The possible explanations for the differences in comorbid disorders may be the qualitative differences in demographics between the two groups. The participants in the dual diagnosis group had higher risk of brain damage caused by teratogens (O'Malley, 2007) and more risk factors (e.g., lower SES and more out-of-home placements) than the single diagnosis group. Research suggests that low SES and out-of-home placements are reported to be risk factors for developing disruptive behavior disorders (e.g., Schonberg & Shaw, 2007). Additionally, among children with ADHD, lower SES was known to predict impulsivity as well as defiance and aggression (Ruf, Schmidt, Lemery-Chalfant, & Goldsmith, 2008), which can be characteristics of disruptive disorders.

The two groups also differed significantly with regard to characteristics specific to presence of ADHD subtypes. In the single ADHD diagnosis group, the predominantly inattentive type and the combined type were most common (each reported

71

approximately 30% of the sample). In contrast, more than half in the dual diagnosis group were the combined type. In particular, the high percentage of the combined type in the dual diagnosis group does not support previous research. For example, findings from the study by Levy, Hay, Bennett, and McStephen (2005) conducted with a community sample of children aged 4-18 years (M_{age} for males =10.75 years, females = 10.52 years) for the appearance rate of ADHD subtypes showed that the percentage of Inattentive type (9.9% of the entire community) was the highest, followed by the combined type (5.8%) and the hyperactive-impulsive type (3.0%) for males. Females exhibited the same trend although lower rates of the Inattentive (4.2%), Combined (2.0%), and Hyperactive-Impulsive (1.7%) subtypes than their male counterparts. Interestingly, the male to female ratio in the present study was approximately 3:1 in the single diagnosis group and 2:1 in the dual diagnosis group, although the difference between the two groups was not statistically significant. In summary, the two groups in the present study were qualitatively different regarding risk/protective factors (e.g., SES), exposure to teratogens, and proportions of ADHD subtypes.

Potential Indicators for Identifying Children with Dual FASD and ADHD Diagnosis Group

Adaptive functioning

What are the differences in adaptive functioning between the dual diagnosis group and the single diagnosis group? The hypothesis that the dual diagnosis group would exhibit more significant difficulties, particularly in the area of socialization, than the single diagnosis group, was not supported in this study. This finding contradicted previous study reporting that children with FASD exhibited significant difficulties in the area of socialization, particularly interpersonal and recreation and leisure time (Whaley

72

et al., 2001). Even though children with ADHD are similar to children with FASD, children with ADHD are known to exhibit difficulties in adaptive functioning (e.g., Stein et al., 1995). Comorbid disorders, however, do not seem to affect the level of the adaptive functioning (Roizen et al., 1994). There were no significant differences between the single and the dual diagnosis groups in the two areas of adaptive functioning.

There are two possible explanations for the nonsignificant differences between the two groups in the area of social interaction and communication. First, even though adaptive functioning scores were available for 175 participants in the dual diagnosis group, only 36 participants in the single diagnosis group had scores on adaptive functioning. Unlike the typical assessment battery for FASD diagnosis that includes assessment of adaptive functioning, assessment battery for ADHD diagnosis does not typically include such an assessment. The low power due to small number of participants in the single diagnosis group may have accounted for the lack of a difference between the two groups on the measure of adaptive functioning. Second, the age range of the participants in the present study was 8-14 year-old, which was lower than that in previous studies. Whaley et al. (2001) reported that the impairment in adaptive functioning may become salient as children with FASD get older. As such, differences in adaptive functioning between the two groups were not found in the present study and further research that examines the adaptive functioning of older populations (e.g., high school students, young adults) is needed.

Furthermore, the level of cognitive functioning (i.e., FSIQ) affected the level of the adaptive functioning in both social interaction and communication, and community living areas. This result was reasonable because the level of adaptive functioning is usually linked to the level of overall cognitive functioning (Sparrow, Cicchetti, & Balla,

2005). Therefore, it is essential to consider overall cognitive functioning and home environment when examining adaptive functioning of older populations.

Behavioral Characteristics

What are the differences in behavioral characteristics between the dual diagnosis group and the single diagnosis group? The hypotheses that there are differences in behavioral characteristics between the single and the dual diagnosis groups were partially supported. On one hand, the hypothesis that the dual diagnosis group will exhibit significantly more externalizing behavior than the single diagnosis group was met both for parent and teacher ratings. On the other hand, the hypothesis that the single ADHD diagnosis group will exhibit significantly more internalizing behavior was not supported; there were no differences between the two groups regarding internalizing behavior by both parent and teacher ratings.

Considering externalizing behavior, children in the dual diagnosis group exhibited more statistically significant externalizing behaviors (i.e., higher scores) than those in the single diagnosis group based on both parent and teacher ratings. Furthermore, the effect sizes ranged from moderate to large (-0.70 and -0.79, respectively). These results may be due to the qualitative differences in demographics between the two groups. Many participants in the dual diagnosis group were prenatally exposed to alcohol as well as other chemicals such as cocaine and nicotine, suggesting that the participants with dual diagnosis had higher chances of having brain damage (O'Malley, 2007). Additionally, the presence of comorbid disruptive disorders (e.g., conduct disorder, CD; oppositional defiant disorder, ODD) was also significantly related to more externalizing behaviors for both ratings. Given that several items in the Externalizing Problems domain overlap with the diagnostic criteria of disruptive disorders, this finding was not unexpected.

74

With regard to the adjusted *T* scores on externalizing behavior, the adjusted mean parent rating (i.e., CBCL) *T* score of the Externalizing Problems domain for the dual diagnosis group was 72.20, which was extremely above the clinical cut-off point (clinical range: *T* score > 63). The adjusted mean *T* score of the single diagnosis group was 65.24, which was also higher than the average score in the general population (i.e., *T* score of 50), and it also fell within the clinical range. In other words, children in both single diagnosis and dual diagnosis groups in the present study exhibited significant externalizing behavior that was in the clinical range. Namely, their average adjusted score was more than 1 *SD* (i.e., *T* score = 10) above the mean (i.e., *T* score of 50), which is higher than the score for normally developing children. However, when the level of the externalizing behavior is salient and exceeds the clinical cut-off point (i.e., clinical range) the child may also have FASD, which suggests the need for referral to medical professionals for further evaluation of possible FASD. Additionally, teacher ratings (i.e., TRF) revealed similar results although all the *T* scores were not as high as parent ratings. The mean *T* score of the dual diagnosis group was within the clinical range, but the mean *T* score of the single diagnosis group fell within the normal range.

In contrast, there were no statistically significant differences between the two groups in internalizing behavior due to the presence of FASD (i.e., single or dual diagnosis) on the basis of parent and teacher ratings. This nonsignificant result between the two groups contradicted previous findings that children with single ADHD diagnosis exhibited significantly higher internalizing behavior than those with dual diagnosis based on parent ratings (e.g., Coles et al., 1997; Greenbaum et al., 2009). When examining the adjusted *T* scores of the Internalizing Problems of parent ratings (i.e., CBCL), the adjusted mean *T* score for both groups were very similar (65.51 for the single diagnosis group and 66.60 for the dual diagnosis group), and both fell within the clinical range (i.e.,

T score > 63). Same tendency was observed on teacher ratings (i.e., TRF), although none of them fell within the clinical range (59.09 and 61.84, respectively).

One plausible explanation for the present result was the demographic characteristics of children in the dual diagnosis group. That is, children in the dual diagnosis group possibly experienced stressful and traumatic experiences because of unstable/poor home environment (e.g., multiple out-of-home placements, lower SES, possible parental alcohol/chemical dependency), which may have resulted in internalizing problems such as depressive mood and/or formal diagnosis of mood disorders. Additionally, the presence of the comorbid mood disorders was significantly related to more internalizing behavior (i.e., higher scores). This finding was understandable given that several diagnostic criteria of mood disorders overlap with items that measure internalizing behavior in both the CBCL and TRF.

Another trend observed in the present study for both externalizing and internalizing behaviors was that parents tended to report more problems than teachers. This finding was similar to the study by Schonfeld et al. (2006) even when they used a different behavior rating scale (i.e., Social Skills Rating System). Parents tended to report more problems (e.g., lack of social skills) than teachers. This difference in parent and teacher ratings may be explained by the fact that some of the teachers in the present study reported knowing the student for less than three months and consequently reported no problems.

Academic Performance

What are the differences in academic performance between the dual diagnosis group and the single diagnosis group? The hypothesis that the dual diagnosis group would perform significantly higher on reading than the single diagnosis group was not

76

supported; there was no statistically significant difference between the two groups in overall reading or mathematics. Moreover, the hypothesis that the dual diagnosis group would perform significantly lower than the single diagnosis group on mathematics was not supported. In contrast, FSIQ and the presence of comorbid learning disorders (LD) were significantly related to the overall reading and mathematics achievement. In other words, children with ADHD exhibit difficulty in reading and/or mathematics when they also have LD and/or lower level of cognitive functioning (i.e., FSIQ), regardless of the presence of FASD. Latter results were understandable, because FSIQ is known to be correlated with overall academic achievement (Woodcock et al., 2001). Additionally, the definition of LD includes "achievement ... is substantially below that expected given the person's chronological age, measured intelligence, and age-appropriate education" (American Psychiatric Association, 2000). Namely, the presence of LD is highly relevant to low overall reading and mathematics achievement. In other words, it is likely that children with FASD who also have ADHD receive special education services under the category of learning disabilities (although medical and educational LD have similar but different criterion) no matter whether they have formal FASD diagnosis or not.

In the area of overall reading achievement, there was no difference between the two groups, contradicting the hypothesis based on the previous study findings that children with ADHD perform significantly poorer than children with FASD in reading (Coles et al., 1997). A possible explanation for the lack of statistically significant differences between the two groups in reading may be the age of the participants. In the present study with age range of 8-14 years old, there was no effect of age on overall reading achievement. However, for children with ADHD, difficulties in reading become less severe as they get older (Frazier et al., 2007). In contrast, for children with FASD, the academic difficulties become more severe as they age (Streissguth et al., 1991).

77

Namely, the difference between the two groups may become more salient after they enter high school (i.e., 15-year-old or older). Thus, it is necessary to further investigate the relation between age and reading achievement in older population (e.g., high school students).

With regard to mathematics achievement, the presence of FASD was not significantly related to overall mathematics achievement. There were only approximately 2.5 points (adjusted) difference on overall mathematics between the two groups; moreover, the adjusted mean scores of the dual diagnosis group were within the low-average range (i.e., within 1 *SD* from the mean; 91.73), indicating that their achievement level is still within the age-appropriate range. Similar to reading achievement, one possible reason for this nonsignificant difference between the two groups on overall mathematics achievement can be explained by the age of the participants. In a study of 512 children with prenatal alcohol exposure whose mean age was 6.5 years old, Goldschmidt et al. (1996) also reported the low-average level in mathematics skills. In contrast, two studies with adolescents (age range: 14-16 years) with FASD showed the mean mathematics score to be more than 1 *SD* from the mean, with significant discrepancy between cognitive level and mathematics achievement (e.g., Olson et al., 1998; Howell et al., 2006). In the present study (age range: 8-14 years), where the age range of children in the present study fell in between early elementary school age (i.e., 6.5 years) and adolescence (i.e., 14-16 years), older age was significantly related to the lower overall mathematics achievement. Therefore, it can be assumed that the difficulties in mathematics become apparent after entering middle school. In other words, it may not be helpful to use mathematics performance to identify differences between the single ADHD diagnosis group and the dual ADHD and FASD diagnosis group in elementary school, but maybe critical after middle school.

78

Study Limitations and Implications for Future Research

Of the studies directly comparing children with FASD and children with ADHD who were not prenatally exposed to alcohol, the present study included a relatively large sample size (N = 338). This large sample could have made it possible to detect subtle but important effects of alcohol on child development and also reduced the impact of participants' individual characteristics. Because this study replicates previous studies, it may allow for generalization of results to the broader population of children with FASD and ADHD. However, there are several limitations of this study that require caution in interpreting the findings. These include a failure to differentiate the effect of alcohol and other chemicals on fetus, selection of participants, limited number of available data for a particular assessment, and generalizability of the present findings to the overall ADHD population.

One limitation of the present study was that it was not clear whether the differences between the single diagnosis group and the dual diagnosis group were due to prenatal alcohol exposure or other chemical exposure. Teratogens such as cocaine and cigarettes are known to affect children's cognitive functioning and behavior (e.g., Bendersky & Lewis, 1998; Chasnoff et al., 1998; O'Connor et al., 2002; Wasserman et al., 1998; Williams et al., 1998). Since the majority of participants in the dual diagnosis group were either exposed or possibly exposed to chemicals during pregnancy, it was impossible to differentiate the impact of alcohol exposure from those of chemical exposure. However, for the purpose of this present study, which is to identify children with the dual ADHD and FASD diagnosis among children with ADHD, these findings are useful because most of the children with FASD were also exposed to chemicals. At the same time, future research is warranted to investigate the impact of teratogens on the

79

development of children who are not prenatally exposed to alcohol, but are exposed to other teratogens (e.g., drugs, nicotine, and caffeine). Findings from this type of research would help identify children who are exposed to other teratogens but do not have FASD early so that they can receive necessary intervention and supports.

A second limitation was the selection of participants in the study. To receive a diagnosis of FASD, the documentation of a confirmed alcohol exposure during pregnancy was required, unless a child had FAS that included all three of the unique FAS facial abnormalities as well as growth deficits and CNS abnormalities (Hoyme et al., 2005). Therefore, the sample excluded many children who might have FASD, but did not receive FASD diagnosis due to a lack of confirmed alcohol exposure during pregnancy. Considering the fact that many of children with FASD in the present study actually experienced several out-of-home placements, the chances are that a number of children could not receive FASD diagnosis due to lack of documentation of prenatal alcohol exposure. It is important to note that the likelihood of obtaining documentation for confirmed alcohol exposure is low. Nevertheless, whether the children have a formal diagnosis of FASD or not, all children with actual FASD are in need of appropriate supports. Future studies that examine methods to identify these children with undiagnosed FASD would be warranted.

A third limitation was that the method of data collection was based on the review of existing medical records. Although this data collection method was efficient and did not require time and resources to administer assessments to participants, data on adaptive functioning was not available for all participants, particularly those in the single diagnosis group because adaptive functioning was not included in the standard assessment battery for those who came to the clinic for ADHD evaluation. Thus, future research that replicates this study should ensure that data in all areas of interests (e.g., adaptive functioning, academic performance) are collected to adequately inform research. Additionally, because all the data were collected at a clinic, the target population of the present study was limited to children with ADHD and/or FASD who came to the clinic to receive a formal medical diagnosis. Although it is difficult to conduct studies on children with ADHD and FASD in schools because they both require diagnoses made by medical professionals, further examination of the difference between the single diagnosis group and the dual diagnosis group in school settings would provide important findings for identifying children with possible FASD by educators.

An additional limitation is the generalizability of the present study findings. The percentages of participants with disruptive disorders in both groups were lower than is commonly reported for those with ADHD (60%, namely 25% for CD and 35% for ODD) by the American Academy of Pediatrics (2000), suggesting that participants in this study may not be an accurate representation of the ADHD population. One study that examined younger children (i.e., first to fourth graders) with ADHD in the community samples reported a lower rate of comorbid disruptive disorders, which was approximately 45% (12% for CD and 32% for ODD; August, Realmuto, McDonald, Nugent, & Crosby, 1996), and this percentage was similar to the percentage of comorbid disruptive disorders in the dual diagnosis group. However, the percentage of those who exhibited disruptive disorders in the single diagnosis group was still lower than 45% (i.e., 20%). Therefore, it is unclear if the current findings on externalizing behavior can be generalized to the broader ADHD population. At the same time, it is important to note that the significant differences on the level of externalizing behavior between groups were consistently observed in multiple settings (i.e., home and school). Future studies that replicate the present study in different areas/settings will reveal the generalizability of the current findings.

The aim of the present study was to examine whether adaptive functioning, behavioral characteristics, and academic performance can be used to explore potential indicators of children with dual diagnosis of FASD and ADHD among children with single ADHD diagnosis. Of the three areas, it seemed that behavioral characteristics, especially externalizing behaviors of the dual diagnosis group become salient at the earliest age. Moreover, it appeared that lowered adaptive functioning, particularly the area of community living, can be detected early. Therefore, further examination of the difference in externalizing behavior and community living skills between the two groups may provide clues for identifying children with dual ADHD and FASD diagnosis among children with ADHD.

References

Aase, J. M., Jones, K. L., & Clarren, S. K. (1995). Do we need the term "FAE"? *Pediatrics, 95*, 428-430.

Abel, E. L. (1999). Was the fetal alcohol syndrome recognized by the Greeks and Romans? *Alcohol and Alcoholism, 34*, 868-872.

Abel, E. L., & Hannigan, J. H. (1996). Risk factors and pathogenesis. In H. L. Spohr & H. C. Steinhausen (Eds.), *Alcohol, pregnancy and the developing child* (pp. 63-75). Cambridge: Cambridge University Press.

Achenbach, T. M. (1991a). *Manual for the Child Behavior Checklist/4-18 and 1991 Profile.* Burlington: University of Vermont Department of Psychiatry.

Achenbach, T. M. (1991b) *Manual for the Teacher's Report Form and 1991 Profile.* Burlington,VT: University of Vermont Department of Psychiatry.

Achenbach, T. M. & Rescorla, L. (2001). *Manual for ASEBA School-Age Forms and Profiles.* Burlington, VT: University of Vermont, Research Center for Children, Youth & Families.

American Academy of Pediatrics. (1996). *The classification of child and adolescent mental diagnoses in primary care: Diagnostic and statistical manual for primary care (DSM-PC) child and adolescent version.* Elk Grove Village, IL: Author.

American Academy of Pediatrics. (2000). Clinical practice guideline: diagnosis and evaluation of the child with attention-deficit/hyperactivity disorder. *Pediatrics, 105*, 1158-1170.

American Association on Mental Retardation. (2002). *Mental retardation: Definition, classification and systems of supports* (10th ed.). Washington Dc: Author.

American Psychiatric Association. (2000). *Diagnostic and statistical manual of mental disorders* (4th ed. text revision). Washington DC: Author.

Astley, S. J., & Clarren, S.K. (2000). Diagnosing the full spectrum of fetal alcohol-exposed individuals: introducing the 4-digit diagnostic code. *Alcohol, 35,* 400-410.

Astley, S. J., Magnuson, S. I., Omnell, L. M., & Clarren, S. K. (1999). Fetal alcohol syndrome: changes in craniofacial form with age, cognition, and timing of ethanol exposure in the macaque. *Teratology, 59,* 163-172.

August, G. J., Realmuto, G. M., MacDonald, A. W., Nugent, S. M., & Crosby, R. (1996). Prevalence of ADHD and comorbid disorders among elementary school children screened for disruptive behavior. *Journal of Abnormal Child Psychology, 24*(5), 571-595.

Barkley, R. A. (2006). *Attention-deficit hyperactivity disorder: a handbook for diagnosis and treatment* (3rd .ed.). New York: Guilford Press.

Barkley, R.A., DuPaul, G. J., & McMurray, M. B. (1990). A comprehensive evaluation of attention deficit disorder with and without hyperactivity. *Journal of Consulting and Clinical Psychology, 58,* 775-789.

Barkley, R. A., Fischer, M., Edelbrock, C., & Smallish, L. (1991). The adolescent outcome of hyperactive children diagnosed by research criteria: III. Mother-child interactions, family conflicts and maternal psychopathology. *Journal of Child Psychology and Psychiatry, 32,* 233-255.

Barkley, R. A., Fischer, M., Smallish, L., & Fletcher, K. (2002). The persistence of attention-deficit/hyperactivity disorder into young adulthood as a function of reporting source and definition of disorder. *Journal of Abnormal Psychology, 111,* 279-289.

Baron, R. M., & Kenny, D. A. (1986). The moderator-mediator variable distinction in social psychological research: Conceptual, strategic, and statistical considerations.

Journal of personality and social psychology, 51(6), 1173 -1182 doi:

http://dx.doi.org.floyd.lib.umn.edu/10.1037/0022-3514.51.6.1173

Bendersky, M., & Lewis, M. (1998). Prenatal cocaine exposure and impulse control at two years. *Annuals of the New York Academy of Sciences, 846*, 365-367.

Bertrand, J., Floyd, R. L., Weber, M. K., O'Connor, M., Riley, E. P., Johnson, K. A., et al. (2004). *National task force on FAS/FAE. Fetal alcohol syndrome: Guidelines for referral and diagnosis.* Atlanta, GA: Centers for Disease Control and Prevention.

Bhatara, V., Loudenberg, R., & Ellis, R. (2006). Association of attention deficit hyperactivity disorder and gestational alcohol exposure: an exploratory study. *Journal of Attention Disorders, 9*, 515-522.

Biederman, J., Ball, S. W., Monuteaux, M. C., Kaiser, R., & Faraone, S. V. (2008). CBCL Clinical Scales discriminate ADHD youth with structured-interview derived diagnosis of oppositional defiant disorder (ODD). *Journal of Attention Disorders, 12*, 76-82.

Biederman, J., & Faraone, S. V. (2002). Current concepts on the neurobiology of Attention-Deficit/Hyperactivity Disorder. *Journal of Attention Disorders, 6*, S7-16.

Biederman, J., Faraone, S., Milberger, S., & Guite, J. (1996). A prospective 4-year follow-up study of attention-deficit hyperactivity and related disorders. *Archives of General Psychiatry, 53*, 437-446.

Bonthius, D. J., Goodlett, C. R., & West, J. R. (1988). Blood alcohol concentration and severity of microencephaly in neonatal rats depend on the pattern of alcohol administration. *Alcohol, 5*, 209-214.

Brown, R. T., Coles, C. D., Smith, I. E., Platzman, K. A., Silverstein, J., Erickson, S., et al. (1991). Effects of prenatal alcohol exposure at school age. II. Attention and behavior. *Neurotoxicology & Teratology, 13*, 369-376.

Bruininks, R. H., Woodcock, R. W., Weatherman, R. F., & Hill, B. K. (1996). *Scales of Independent Behavior-Revised (SIB-R) manual.* Rolling Meadows, IL: Riverside.

Burd, L., Klug, M. G., Martsolf, J. T., & Kerbeshian, J. (2003). Fetal alcohol syndrome: neuropsychiatric phenomics. *Neurotoxicology & Teratology, 25,* 697-705.

Burden, M. J., Jacobson, S. W., & Jacobson, J. L. (2005a). Relation of prenatal alcohol exposure to cognitive processing speed and efficiency in childhood. *Alcoholism: Clinical & Experimental Research, 29,* 1473-1483.

Centers for Disease Control. (2002). Alcohol use among women of childbearing age: United States, 1991–1999. *Morbidity and Mortality Weekly Report, 51,* 273–276.

Chen, W.J., Faraone, S. V., Biederman, J., & Tsuang, M. T. (1994). Diagnostic accuracy of the Child Behavior Checklist scales for attention-deficit hyperactivity disorder: A receiver-operating characteristic analysis. *Journal of Consulting and Clinical Psychology, 62,* 1017-1025.

Christoffel, K. K., & Salafsky, I. (1975). Fetal alcohol syndrome in dizygotic twins. *Journal of Pediatrics, 87,* 963-967.

Coggins, T., Friet, T., & Morgan, T. (1998). Analyzing narrative productions in older school-age children and adolescents with fetal alcohol syndrome: An experimental tool for clinical applications. *Clinical Linguistics & Phonetics, 12,* 221-236.

Cohen, J (1992). A power primer. *Psychological Bulletin, 112,* 155–159. doi:10.1037/0033-2909.112.1.155.

Cohen, J., & Cohen, P. (1983). *Applied multiple regression/correlation analysis for the behavioral sciences* (2nd ed.). Hillsdale, NJ: Lawrence Erlbaum Associates.

Cohen, L. G., Spenciner, L. J. (2006). *Assessment of children and youth with special needs (3rd ed.).* Boston: Pearson.

Coles, C. D., Platzman, K. A., Raskind-Hood, C. L., Brown, R. T., Falek, A., & Smith, I. E. (1997). A comparison of children affected by prenatal alcohol exposure and attention deficit, hyperactivity disorder. *Alcoholism: Clinical and Experimental Research, 21*(1), 150-161. doi: 10.1111/j.1530-0277.1997.tb03743.x

Coles, C. D., Smith, I., Fernhoff, P. M., & Falek, A. (1985). Neonatal neurobehavioral characteristics as correlates of maternal alcohol use during gestation. *Alcoholism: Clinical and Experimental Research, 9*, 454-460.

Connor, D. F. (2006). Stimulants. In R. A. Berkley (Ed.), *Attention-deficit hyperactivity disorder: a handbook for diagnosis and treatment* (3rd ed., pp. 608-647). New York: Guilford Press.

D'Agostino, R. B., Jr. (1998). Propensity Score Methods for Bias Reduction in the Comparison of a Treatment to a Non-Randomized Control Group. *Statistics in Medicine, 17*(19), 2265-2281.

Dawkins, M. P., & Harper, F. D. (1983). Alcoholism among women: A comparison of Black and White problem drinkers. *International Journal of the Addictions, 18*, 333-349.

Day, N. L., Robles, N., Richardson, G., Geva, D., Taylor, P., Scher, M. et al. (1991). The effects of prenatal alcohol use on the growth of children at three years of age. *Alcoholism: Clinical and Experimental Research, 15*, 67-71.

Dunn, O.J. (1961). Multiple Comparisons Among Means. *Journal of the American Statistical Association, 56*, 52-64.

DuPaul, G. J., & Stoner, G. (2003). *ADHD in the schools: Assessment and intervention strategies (2nd ed.).* New York: Guilford Press.

Dupere, V., Leventhal, T., Crosnoe, R., & Dion, E. (2010). Understanding the Positive Role of Neighborhood Socioeconomic Advantage in Achievement: The Contribution of the Home, Child Care, and School Environments. *Developmental Psychology, 46*(5), 1227–1244.

Eiraldi, R. B., Power, T. J., Karustis, J. L., & Goldstein, S. G. (2000). Assessing ADHD and comorbid disorders in children: The Child Behavior Checklist and the Devereux Scales of Mental Disorders. *Journal of Clinical Child Psychology, 29*, 3-16.

Ernhart, C. B., Morrow-Tlucak, M., Sokol, R, J., & Martier, S. (1988). Underreporting of alcohol use in pregnancy. *Alcoholism: Clinical and Experimental Research, 12*, 506-511.

Fast, D. K., Conry, J., & Loock, C. A. (1999). Identifying fetal alcohol syndrome among youth in the criminal justice system. *Journal of Developmental & Behavioral Pediatrics, 20*, 370-372.

Fergusson, D. M., & Horwood, L. J. (1993). The structure, stability and correlations of the trait components of conduct disorder, attention deficit and anxiety/withdrawal reports. *Journal of Child Psychology and Psychiatry, 34*, 749-766.

Farrington, D., Loeber, R., & van Kammen, W. B. (1990). Long-term outcome of hyperactivity-impulsivity-attention deficit problems in childhood. In L. N. Robins & M. Rutter (Eds.), *Straight and devious pathways from childhood to adulthood* (pp. 62-81). Cambridge: Cambridge University Press.

Frazier, T. W., Demaree, H. A., & Youngstrom, E. A. (2004). Meta-analysis of intellectual and neuropsychological test performance in attention-deficit/hyperactivity disorder. *Neuropsychology, 18*, 543-555.

Frazier, T. W., Youngstrom, E. A., Glutting, J. J., & Watkins, M. W. (2007). ADHD and achievement: Meta-analysis of the child, adolescent, and adult literatures and a concomitant study with college students. *Journal of Learning Disabilities, 40,* 49-65.

Friend, M. (2010). *Special Education: Contemporary Perspectives for School Professionals*, (3rd ed.). Upper Saddle River, NJ: Pearson.

Fryer, S. L., McGee, C. L., Matt, G. E., Riley, E. P., & Mattson, S. N. (2007). Evaluation of psychopathological conditions in children with heavy prenatal alcohol exposure. *Pediatrics, 119*, e733-741.

Gardner, J. (2000). Living with a child with fetal alcohol syndrome. *American Journal of Maternanl/Child Nursing, 25*, 252.

Greenbaum, R. L., Stevens, S. A., Nash, K., Koren, G., & Rovet, J. (2009). Social Cognitive and Emotion Processing Abilities of Children With Fetal Alcohol Spectrum Disorders: A Comparison With Attention Deficit Hyperactivity Disorder. *Alcoholism: Clinical and Experimental Research, 33*(10), 1656-1670. doi:10.1111/j.1530-0277.2009.01003.x

Gresham, F. M., & Elliott, S. N. (1993). *Social Skills Rating System manual.* Circle Pines, MN: AGS.

Gold, S., & Sherry, L. (1984). Hyperactivity, learning disabilities, and alcohol. *Journal of Learning Disabilities, 17*, 3-6.

Goldschmidt, L., Richardson, G. A., Stoffer, D. S., Geva, D., & Day, N. L. (1996). Prenatal alcohol exposure and academic achievement at age six: A nonlinear fit. *Alcoholism: Clinical & Experimental Research, 20*, 763-770.

Halmesmaki, E. (1988). Alcohol counselling of 85 pregnant problem drinkers: effect on drinking and fetal outcome. *British Journal of Obstetrics & Gynaecology, 95*, 243-247.

Hansen, R.L., Mawjee, F.L., Barton, K., Metcalf, M.B., & Joye, N.R. (2004). Comparing the health status of low-income children in and out of foster care. *Child Welfare: Journal of Policy, Practice, and Program, 83*(4), 367-380.

Harwood, H.J., & Napolitano, D.M., Kristiansen, P., & Collins, J. J. (1984). *Economic Costs to Society of Alcohol and Drug Abuse and Mental Illness: 1980*. Research Triangle Park, NC: Research Triangle Institute.

Hill, R. B. (2005). The role of race in foster care placement. In D. Derezotes, J. Poetner, & M. Testa (Eds.), *Race matters in child welfare: The overrepresentation of African American children in the system* (pp. 187–200). Washington, DC: Child Welfare League of America.

Holm, S. (1979). A simple sequentially rejective multiple test procedure. *Scandinavian Journal of Statistics, 6*(2), 65-70.

Howell, D. C. (2001). *Statistical methods for psychology* (5th ed.). Belmont, CA: Wadsworth Publishing.

Howell, K. K., Lynch, M. E., Platzman, K. A., Smith, G. H., & Coles, C. D. (2006). Prenatal alcohol exposure and ability, academic achievement, and school functioning in adolescence: A longitudinal follow-up. *Journal of Pediatric Psychology, 31*, 116-126.

Hoyme, H. E., May, P. A., Kalberg, W. O., Kodituwakku, P., Gossage, J. P., Trujillo, P. M., et al. (2005). A practical clinical approach to diagnosis of fetal alcohol spectrum disorders: clarification of the 1996 institute of medicine criteria. *Pediatrics, 115*, 39-47.

Institute of Medicine. (1996). *Fetal alcohol syndrome: Diagnosis, epidemiology, prevention, and treatment*. Washington, DC: National Academy Press.

Jacobson, J. L., & Jacobson, S. W. (2005). Methodological issues in research on developmental exposure to neurotoxic agents. *Neurotoxicology and Teratology, 27*, 395-406.

Jacobson, S. W., & Jacobson, J. L. (1992). Early exposure to PCBs and other suspected teratogens: assessment of coufounding (pp. 135-154). In C. W. Greenbaum, & J. G. Auerbach (Eds.), *Longitudinal studies of children at risk: cross-national perspectives.* Norwood, NJ: Ablex.

Jacobson, S. W., Jacobson, J. L., Sokol, R. J., Chiodo, L. M., & Corobana, R. (2004). Maternal age, alcohol abuse history, and quality of parenting as moderators of the effects of prenatal alcohol exposure on 7.5-year intellectual function. *Alcoholism: Clinical & Experimental Research, 28*, 1732-1745.

Jester, J. M., Jacobson, S. W., Sokol, R. J., Tuttle, B. S., & Jacobson, J. L. (2000). The influence of maternal drinking and drug use on the quality of the home environment of school-aged children. *Alcoholism: Clinical & Experimental Research, 24*, 1187-1197.

Jirikowic, T., Olson, H., &. Kartin, D. (2008). Sensory processing, school performance, and adaptive behavior of young school-age children with fetal alcohol spectrum disorders. *Physical & Occupational Therapy in Pediatrics, 28*, 117-136.

Jones, K. L. (1997). Smith's Recognizable Patterns of Human Malformation (5th ed.). Philadelphia, PA: W. B. Saunders.

Kopera-Frye, K., Dehaene, S., & Streissguth, A. P. (1996). Impairments of number processing induced by prenatal alcohol exposure. *Neuropsychologia, 34*, 1187-1196.

LaDue, R. A., Streissguth, A. P., & Randels, S. P. (1992). *Perinatal substance abuse: Research findings and clinical implications.* Baltimore, MD: John Hopkins University Press.

Levy, F., Hay, D. A., Bennett, K. S., & McStephen, M. (2005). Gender Differences in ADHD Subtype Comorbidity. *Journal of the American Academy of Child & Adolescent Psychiatry, 44*(4), 368-376. doi:10.1097/01.chi.0000153232.64968.c1

Linnet, K. M., Dalsgaard, S., Obel, C., Wisborg, K., Henriksen, T. B., Rodriguez, A., et al. (2003). Maternal lifestyle factors in pregnancy risk of attention deficit hyperactivity disorder and associated behaviors: review of the current evidence. *American Journal of Psychiatry, 160*, 1028-1040.

Lupton, C., Burd, L., & Harwood, R. (2004). Cost of fetal alcohol spectrum disorders. *American Journal of Medical Genetics, 127C*(1), 42-50. doi:10.1002/ajmg.c.30015

Merriam-Webster's collegiate dictionary (11th ed.). (2003). Springfield, MA: Merriam-Webster.

Maesten, A. S. (2001). Ordinary magic: Resilience processes in development. *American Psychologist, 56*, 227-238.

Maesten, A. S., & Garmezy, N. (1985). Risk, vulnerability, and protective factors in the developmental psychopathology. In B. B. Lahey & A. E. Kazdin (Eds.), *Advances in clinical child psychology* (Vol. 8, pp. 1-51). New York: Plenum.

Maesten, A.S., &Wright, M. O. D. (1998). Cumulative risk and protection models of child maltreatment. In B. B. R. Rossman & M. S. Rosenberg (Eds.), *Multiple victimization of children: Conceptual, developmental, research and treatment issues* (pp. 7-30). Binghamton, NY: Haworth.

Manikam, R., Matson, J. L., Coe, D. A., & Hillman, N. (1995). Adolescent depression: relationships of self-report to intellectual and adaptive functioning. *Research in Developmental Disabilities, 16*, 349-364.

Mariani, M. A., & Barkley, R. A. (1997). Neuropsychological and academic functioning in preschool boys with attention deficit hyperactivity disorder. *Developmental Neuropsychology, 13*, 111-129.

May, P. A., & Gossage, J. P. (2001). Estimating the prevalence of fetal alcohol syndrome. A summary. *Alcohol Research & Health: the Journal of the National Institute on Alcohol Abuse & Alcoholism, 25*, 159-167.

Murphy, K., & Barkley, R. A. (1996). Prevalence of DSM-IV symptoms of ADHD in adult licensed drivers: Implications for clinical diagnosis. *Journal of Attention Disorders, 1*, 147-161.

Murphy, K., & Myors, B. (2004). *Statistical power analysis: a simple and general model for traditional and modern hypothesis tests* (2nd.ed.). Mahwah, NJ: Lawrence Erlbaum.

Nanson, J. L., & Hiscock, M. (1990). Attention deficits in children exposed to alcohol prenatally. *Alcoholism: Clinical & Experimental Research, 14*, 656-661.

O'Connor, T. G., Heron, J., Golding, J., Beveridge, M., & Glover, V. (2002). Maternal antenatal anxiety and child\ren's behavioural/emotional problems at 4 years: Report from the Avon Longitudinal Study of Parents and Children. *British Journal of Psychiatry, 180*, 502-508.

Oesterheld, J., & O'Malley, K. D. (1999). Are ADHD and FAS really that similar? *Iceberg, 9*, 1-7.

Olsen, J., Pereira, A. C., & Olsen, S. F. (1991). Does maternal tobacco smoking modify the effect of alcohol on fetal growth? *American Journal of Public Health, 81*, 69-73.

Olson, H. (2002). Helping individuals with fetal alcohol syndrome and related conditions: A clinician's overview. In R. J. McMahon & R. D. Peters (Eds.), *The effects of parental dysfunction on children* (pp. 147-178). New York: Kluwer Academic/Plenum.

Olson, H., Feldman, J. J., Streissguth, A. P., Sampson, P. D., & Bookstein, F. L. (1998). Neuropsychological deficits in adolescents with fetal alcohol syndrome: Clinical findings. *Alcoholism: Clinical and Experimental Research, 22*, 1998-2012.

Olson, H., Streissguth, A. P., Sampson, P. D., Barr, H. M., Bookstein, F. L., & Thiede, K. (1997). Association of prenatal alcohol exposure with behavioral and learning problems in early adolescence. *Journal of the American Academy of Child & Adolescent Psychiatry, 36*, 1187-1194.

O'Malley, K. D. (2007). *ADHD and fetal alcohol spectrum disorders (FASD)*. Hauppauge: NY, Nova Publishers.

O'Malley, K. D., Koplin, B., & Dohner, V. A. (2000). Psychostimulant response in fetal alcohol syndrome. *Canadian Journal of Psychiatry, 45*, 90-91.

O'Malley, K. D., & Nanson, J. (2002). Clinical implications of a link between fetal alcohol disorder and ADHD. *Canadian Journal of Psychiatry, 47,* 349-354.

Paul, R., Looney, S. S., & Dahm, P. S. (1991). Communication and socialization skills at ages 2 and 3 in "late-talking" young children. *Journal of Speech & Hearing Research, 34*, 858-865.

Perneger, Thomas V. (1998). What's wrong with Bonferroni adjustments. *British Medical Journal, 316*, 1236-1238.

Pierce, D. R., & West, J. R. (1986). Alcohol-induced microencephaly during the third trimester equivalent: relationship to dose and blood alcohol concentration. *Alcohol, 3*, 185-191.

Powell, T. W., & Germani, M. J. (1993). Linguistic, intellectual, and adaptive behavior skills in a sample of children with communication disorders. *Journal of Psychoeducational Assessment, 11*, 158-172.

Rasmussen, C., Horne, K., & Witol, A. (2006). Neurobehavioral functioning in children with fetal alcohol spectrum disorder. *Neuropsychology, 12*, 453-468.

Roizen, N.J., Blondis, T. A., Irwin, M., & Stein, M. (1994). Adaptive functioning in
children with attention-deficit hyperactivity disorder. *Archives of Pediatric and
Adolescent Medicine, 148*, 1137-1142.

Rosenbaum, P. R., & Rubin, D. B. (1983). The Central Role of the Propensity Score in
Observational Studies for Causal Effects. *Biometrika 70*, 41-55.

Ruf, H.T., Schmidt, N.L., Lemery-Chalfant, K., & Goldsmith, H. H. (2008). Components
of childhood impulsivity and inattention: Child, family, and genetic correlates.
European Journal of Developmental Science, 2(1-2), 52-76.

Rutter, M. (1981). *Maternal deprivaition reassessed* (2nd ed.). Harmondsworth,
Middlesex, UK: Penguin.

Rutter, M., & Sroufe, L. A. (2000). Developmental psychopathology: Concepts and
challenges. *Development and Psychopathology, 12*, 265-296.

Sattler, J. M. (1992). *Assessment of children*. San Diego, CA: JM Sattler.

Schonberg, M. A., & Shaw, D. S. (2007). Risk Factors for Boy's Conduct Problems in
Poor and Lower–middle-class Neighborhoods. *Journal of Abnormal Child
Psychology, 35*(5), 759-772. doi:10.1007/s10802-007-9125-4

Schonfeld, A. M., Paley, B., Frankel, F., & O'Connor, M. J. (2006). Executive functioning
predicts social skills following prenatal alcohol exposure. *Child Neuropsychology, 12*,
439-452.

Sokol, R. J., Ager, J., Martier, S., Debanne, S., Ernhart, C., Kuzma, J. et al. (1986).
Significant determinants of susceptibility to alcohol teratogenicity. *Annals of the New
York Academy of Sciences, 477*, 87-102.

Sokol, R. J., Smith, M., Ernhart, C. B., Baumann, R., Martier, S. S., Ager, J. W. et al.
(1989). A genetic basis for alcohol-related birth defects (ARBD)? *Alcoholism: Clinical
and Experimental Research, 13*, 343A.

Sparrow, S. S., Cicchetti, D. V., & Balla, D. A. (2005). *Vineland Adaptive Behavior Scales, Second Edition, Manual.* Minneapolis, MN: Pearson.

Speltz, M. L., DeKlyen, M., Calderon, R., Greenberg, M. T., & Fisher, P. A. (1999). Neuropsychological characteristics and test behaviors of boys with early onset conduct problems. *Journal of Abnormal Psychology, 108*, 315-325.

Sroufe, L. A., & Rutter, M. (1984). The domain of developmental psychopathology. *Child Development, 55*, 17-29.

Stein, M. A., Szumowski, E., Blondis, T. A., & Roizen, N. J. (1995). Adaptive skills dysfunction in ADD and ADHD children. *Journal of Child Psychology and Psychiatry, 36*, 663-670.

Steinhausen, H. C., & Spohr, H. L. (1998). Long-term outcome of children with fetal alcohol syndrome: Psychopathology, behavior, and intelligence. *Alcoholism: Clinical and Experimental Research, 22*, 334-338.

Steinhausen, H. C., Willms, J., & Spohr, H. L. (2003). Behavioural phenotype in foetal alcohol syndrome and foetal alcohol effects. *Developmental Medicine & Child Neurology, 45*, 179-182.

Steinhausen, H. C., Metzke, C. W., Meier, M., & Kannenberg, R. (1997). Behavioral and emotional problems reported by parents for ages 6 to 17 in a Swiss epidemiological study. *European Child & Adolescent Psychiatry, 6*, 136-141.

Stinson, F. S., Grant, B. F., Dawson, D. A., Ruan, W., Huang, B., & Saha, T. (2005). Comorbidity between DSM-IV alcohol and specific drug use disorders in the United States: results from the National Epidemiologic Survey on Alcohol and Related Conditions. *Drug and alcohol dependence, 80*(1), 105–116.

Streissguth, A. P., Aase, J. M., Clarren, S. K., Randels, S. P., LaDue, R. A., & Smith, D. F. (1991). Fetal alcohol syndrome in adolescents and adults. *Journal of the American Medical Association. 265*, 1961-1967.

Streissguth, A. P., Barr, H. M., Kogan, J., & Bookstein, F. L. (1996). *Understanding the occurrence of secondary disabilities in clients with fetal alcohol synedrome (FAS) and fetal alcohol effects (FAE): Final report.* Seattle: University of Washington Publication Services.

Streissguth, A. P., Barr, H. M., & Sampson, P. D. (1990). Moderate prenatal alcohol exposure: Effects on child IQ and learning problems at age 71/2 years. *Alcoholism: Clinical and Experimental Research, 14*, 662-669.

Streissguth, A. P., & Kanter, J. (Eds.). (1997). *The challenge of fetal alcohol syndrome: Overcoming secondary disabilities.* Seattle, WA: University of Washington Press.

Substance Abuse and Mental Health Services Administration (2007). *Reach to teach: Educating elementary and middle school students with fetal alcohol spectrum disorders.* Rockville, MD: Center for Substance Abuse Prevention, Substance Abuse and Mental Health Services Administration.

Thomas, S. E., Kelly, S. J., Mattson, S. N., & Riley, E. P. (1998). Comparison of social abilities of children with fetal alcohol syndrome to those of children with similar IQ scores and normal controls. Alcoholism: Clinical & Experimental Research, 22, 528-533.

Tucker, C. M., Chennault, S. A., Brady, B. A., Fraser, K. P, Gaskin, V.T., Dunn, C. et al. (1995). A parent, community, public schools, and university involved partnership education program to examine and boost academic achievement and adaptive functioning skills of African-American students. *Journal of Research & Development in Education, 28*, 174-185.

Vig, S., & Jedrysek, E. (1995). Adaptive behavior of young urban children with developmental disabilities. *Mental Retardation, 33*, 90-98.

Wechsler, D. (2001). *Wechsler Individual Achievement Test- Second edition (WIAT-II) administration and scoring manual.* San Antonio, TX: Pearson.

Wechsler, D. (2003). *Wechsler Intelligence Scale for Children-Fourth edition (WISC–IV) administration and scoring manual.* San Antonio, TX: The Psychological Corporation.

Weinberg, N. Z. (1997). Cognitive and behavioral deficits associated with parental alcohol use. *Journal of the American Academy of Child & Adolescent Psychiatry, 36*, 1177-1186.

Whaley, S. E., O'Connor, M. J., & Gunderson, B. (2001). Comparison of the adaptive functioning of children prenatally exposed to alcohol to a nonexposed clinical sample. *Alcoholism: Clinical and Experimental Research, 25*, 1018-1024.

Wilkinson, G. S., & Robertson, G. J. (2006). Wide Range Achievement Test 4 professional manual. Lutz, FL: Psychological Assessment Resources.

Woodcock, R., McGrew, K. S., & Mather, N. (2001). *Woodcock-Johnson III Tests of Achievement.* Rolling Meadows, IL: Riverside Publishing.

Wright, J. T., Waterson, E. J., Barrison, I. G., Toplis, P. J., Lewis, I. G., Gordon, M. G. et al. (1983). Alcohol consumption, pregnancy, and low birth weight. *Lancet, 1*, 663-665.

Normal Q-Q Plot of Residual for Com_cation

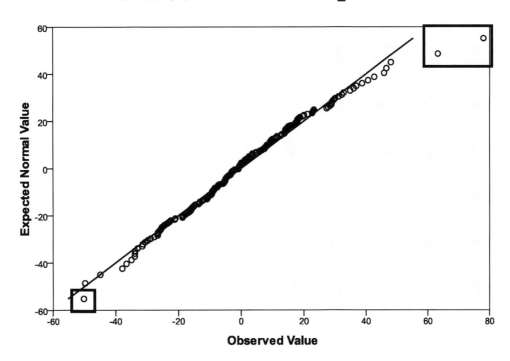

Figure 4.1. Normal Q-Q plot of the Social Interaction and Communication

composite of the Scales of Independent Behavior- Revised (SIB-R). The plots in

bold squares are potential outliers and excluded from the analyses.

Normal Q-Q Plot of Residual for Community

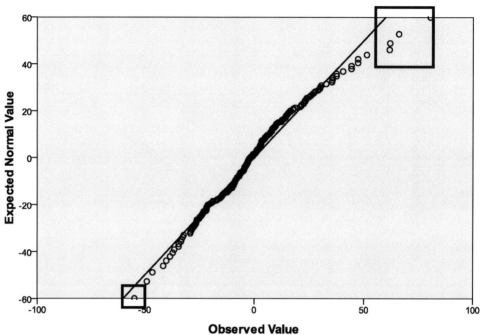

Figure 4.2. Normal Q-Q plot of the Community Living composite of the Scales of

Independent Behavior- Revised (SIB-R). The plots in bold squares are potential

outliers and excluded from the analyses.

100

Normal Q-Q Plot of Residual for Int_CB_sc

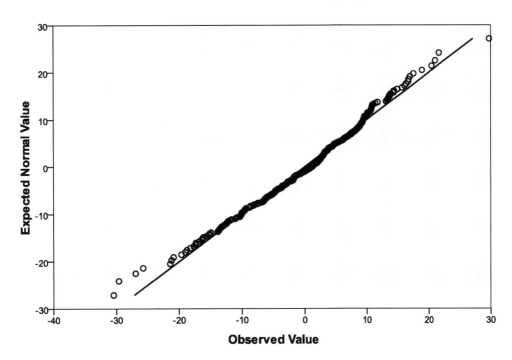

Figure 4.3. Normal Q-Q plot of the Internalizing Behavior of the Child Behavior

Checklist (CBCL).

Normal Q-Q Plot of Residual for Ext_CB_sc

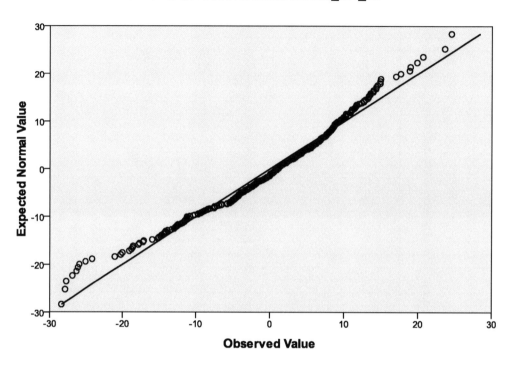

Figure 4.4. Normal Q-Q plot of the Externalizing Behavior of the Child Behavior

Checklist (CBCL).

Normal Q-Q Plot of Residual for Int_TRF_sc

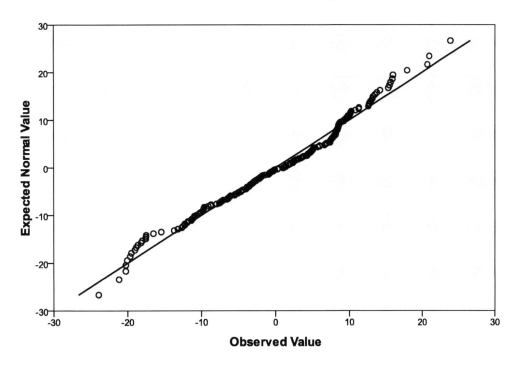

Figure 4.5. Normal Q-Q plot of the Internalizing Behavior of the Teacher Report

Form (TRF).

Normal Q-Q Plot of Residual for Ext_TRF_sc

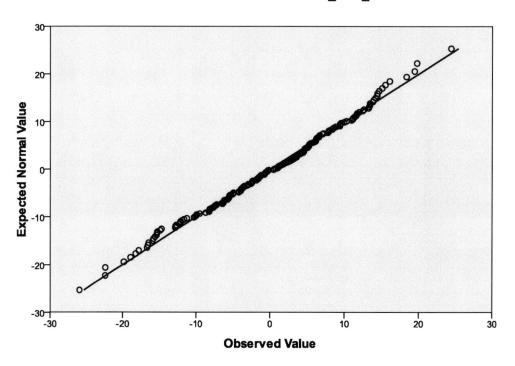

Figure 4.6. Normal Q-Q plot of the Externalizing Behavior of the Teacher Report

Form (TRF).

Normal Q-Q Plot of Residual for Bro_R

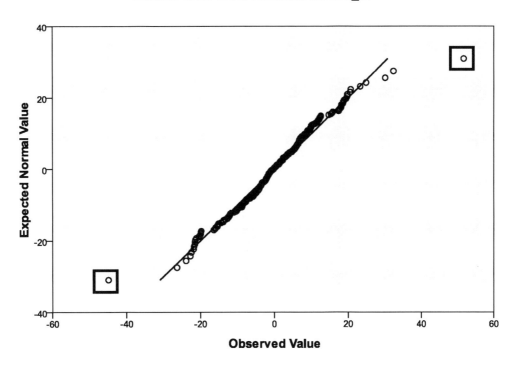

Figure 4.7. Normal Q-Q plot of the Broad Reading composite of the Woodcock

Johnson Test of Achievement- Third Edition (WJ III ACH). The plots in bold

squares are potential outliers and excluded from the analyses.

Normal Q-Q Plot of Residual for Bro_M

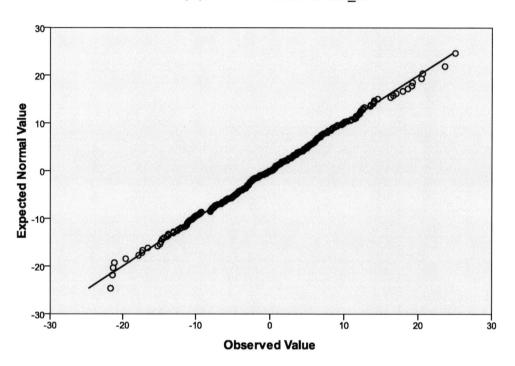

Figure 4.8. Normal Q-Q plot of the Broad Math composite of the Woodcock

Johnson Test of Achievement- Third Edition (WJ III ACH).

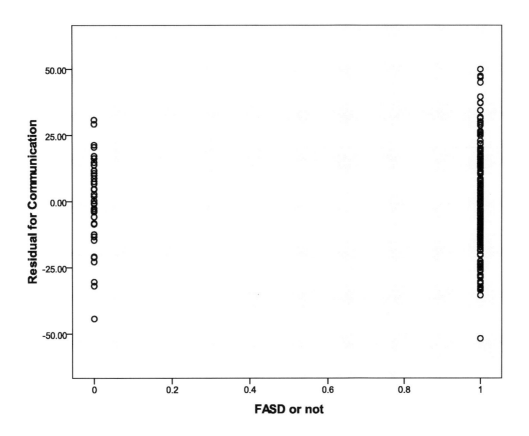

Figure 4.9. Scatter plot of residuals of the Social Interaction and Communication

composite of the Scales of Independent Behavior- Revised (SIB-R) for the

presence of FASD. Similarity on spreads of the scatter plots indicates

homogeneity of variance.

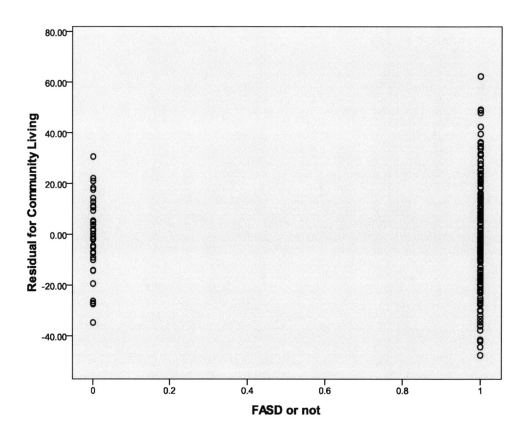

Figure 4.10. Scatter plot of residuals of the Community Living composite of the

Scales of Independent Behavior- Revised (SIB-R) for the presence of FASD.

Similarity on spreads of the scatter plots indicates homogeneity of variance.

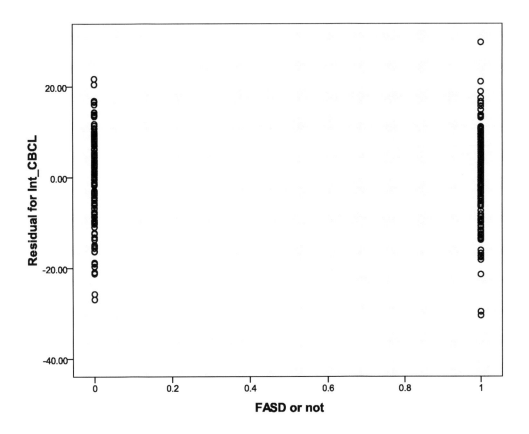

Figure 4.11. Scatter plot of residuals of the Internalizing Behavior of the Child

Behavior Checklist (CBCL) for the presence of FASD. Similarity on spreads of

the scatter plots indicates homogeneity of variance.

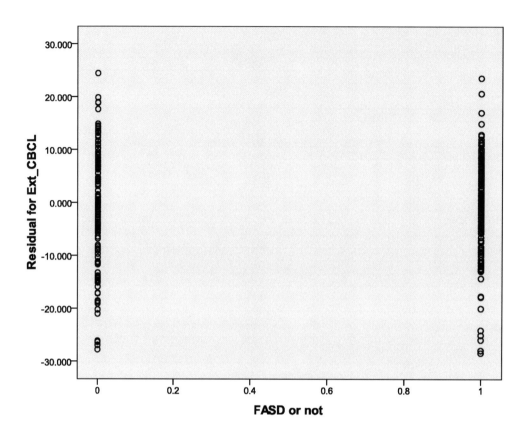

Figure 4.12. Scatter plot of residuals of the Externalizing Behavior of the Child

Behavior Checklist (CBCL) for the presence of FASD. Similarity on spreads of

the scatter plots indicates homogeneity of variance.

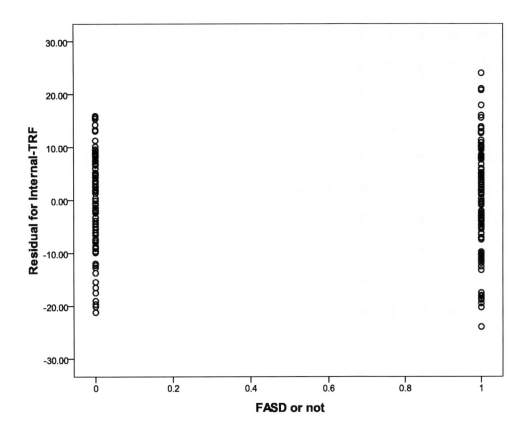

Figure 4.13. Scatter plot of residuals of the Internalizing Behavior of the Teacher Report Form (TRF) for the presence of FASD. Similarity on spreads of the scatter plots indicates homogeneity of variance.

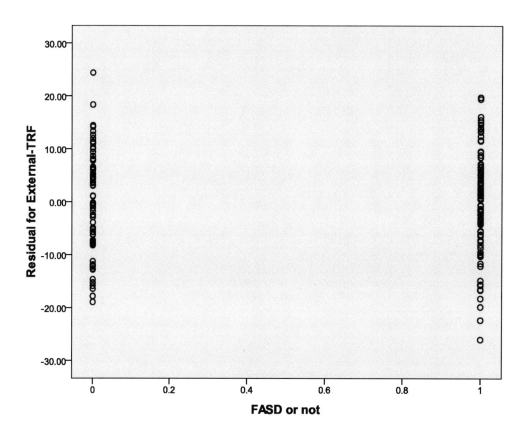

Figure 4.14. Scatter plot of residuals of the Externalizing Behavior of the Teacher

Report Form (TRF) for the presence of FASD. Similarity on spreads of the scatter

plots indicates homogeneity of variance.

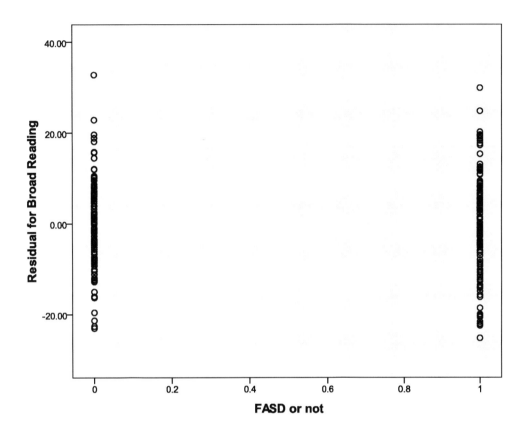

Figure 4.15. Scatter plot of residuals of the Broad Reading composite of the Woodcock Johnson Test of Achievement- Third Edition (WJ III ACH) for the presence of FASD. Similarity on spreads of the scatter plots indicates homogeneity of variance.

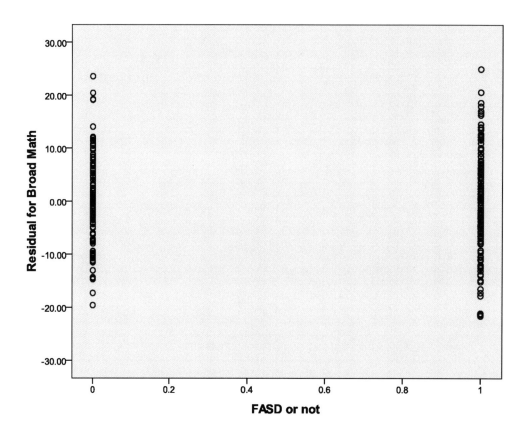

Figure 4.16. Scatter plot of residuals of the Broad Math composite of the

Woodcock Johnson Test of Achievement- Third Edition (WJ III ACH) for the

presence of FASD. Similarity on spreads of the scatter plots indicates

homogeneity of variance.

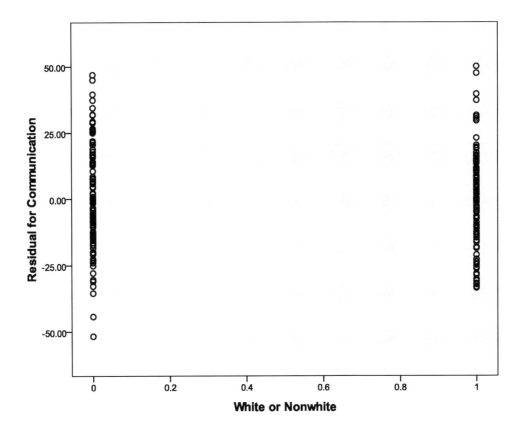

Figure 4.17. Scatter plot of residuals of the Social Interaction and Communication composite of the Scales of Independent Behavior- Revised (SIB-R) for White or nonwhite. Similarity on spreads of the scatter plots indicates homogeneity of variance.

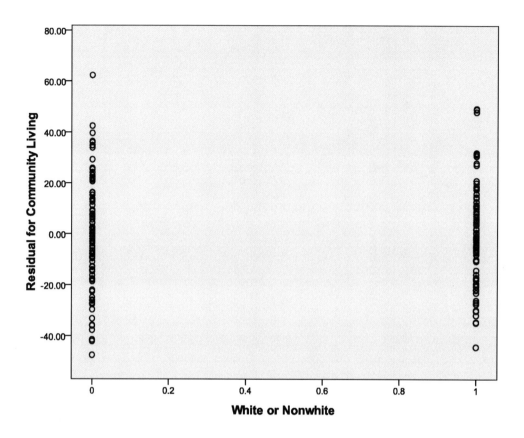

Figure 4.18. Scatter plot of residuals of the Community Living composite of the

Scales of Independent Behavior- Revised (SIB-R) for White or nonwhite.

Similarity on spreads of the scatter plots indicates homogeneity of variance.

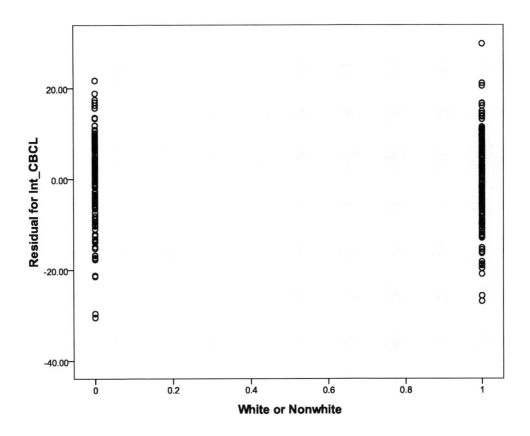

Figure 4.19. Scatter plot of residuals of the Internalizing Behavior of the Child

Behavior Checklist (CBCL) for White or nonwhite. Similarity on spreads of the

scatter plots indicates homogeneity of variance.

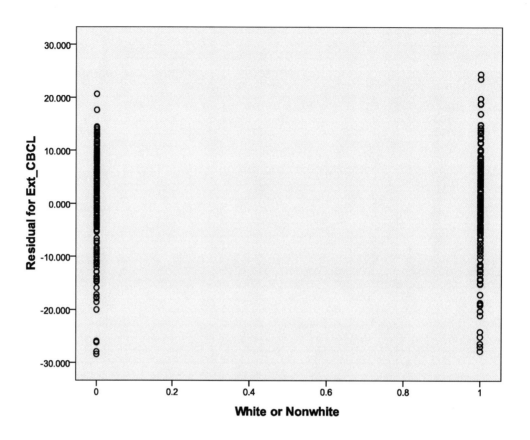

Figure 4.20. Scatter plot of residuals of the Externalizing Behavior of the Child

Behavior Checklist (CBCL) for White or nonwhite. Similarity on spreads of the

scatter plots indicates homogeneity of variance.

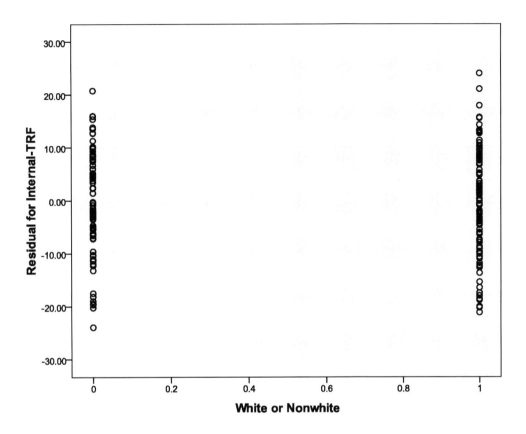

Figure 4.21. Scatter plot of residuals of the Internalizing Behavior of the Teacher

Report Form (TRF) for White or nonwhite. Similarity on spreads of the scatter

plots indicates homogeneity of variance.

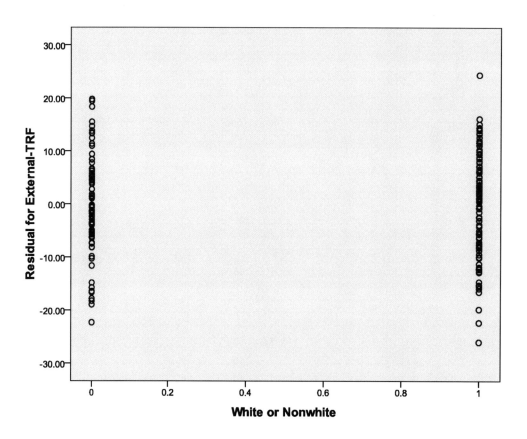

Figure 4.22. Scatter plot of residuals of the Externalizing Behavior of the Teacher

Report Form (TRF) for White or nonwhite. Similarity on spreads of the scatter

plots indicates homogeneity of variance.

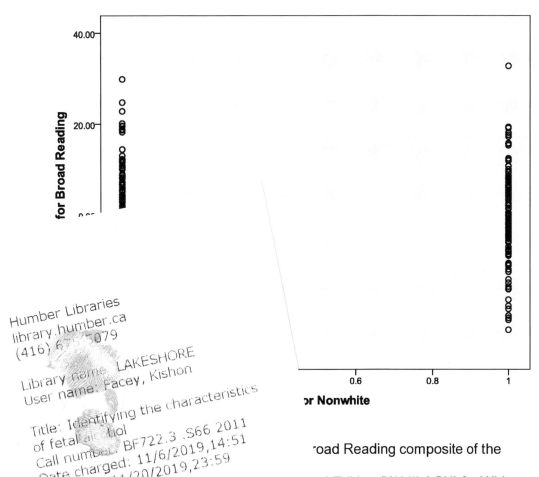

or Nonwhite

road Reading composite of the

d Edition (WJ III ACH) for White or

lots indicates homogeneity of

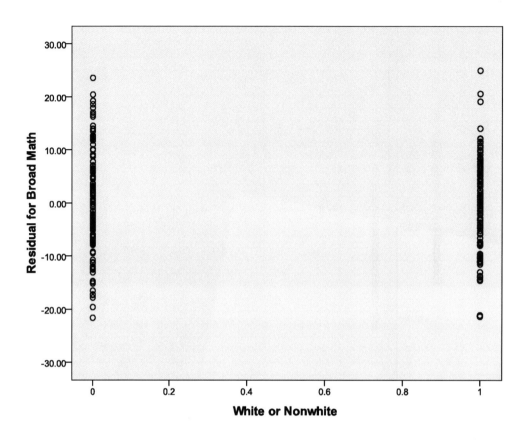

Figure 4.24. Scatter plot of residuals of the Broad Math composite of the

Woodcock Johnson Test of Achievement- Third Edition (WJ III ACH) for White or

nonwhite. Similarity on spreads of the scatter plots indicates homogeneity of

variance.

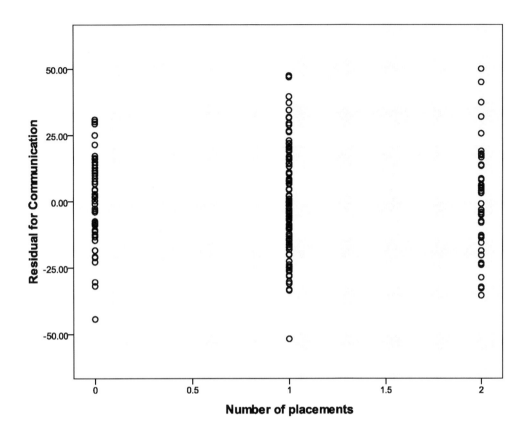

Figure 4.25 Scatter plot of residuals of the Social Interaction and Communication composite of the Scales of Independent Behavior- Revised (SIB-R) for the number of out-of-home placements. Similarity on spreads of the scatter plots indicates homogeneity of variance.

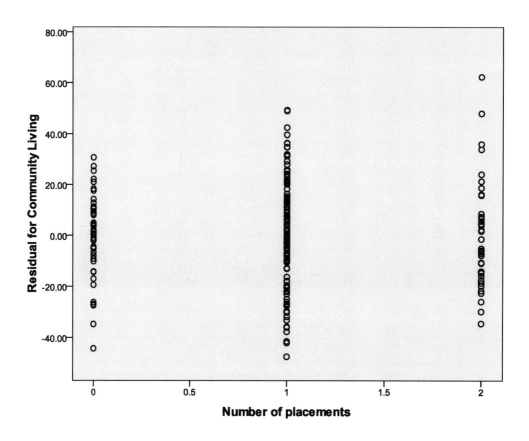

Figure 4.26. Scatter plot of residuals of the Community Living composite of the

Scales of Independent Behavior- Revised (SIB-R) for the number of out-of-home

placements. Similarity on spreads of the scatter plots indicates homogeneity of

variance.

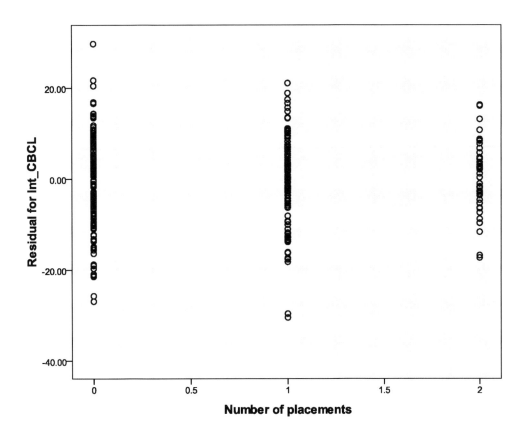

Figure 4.27. Scatter plot of residuals of the Internalizing Behavior of the Child

Behavior Checklist (CBCL) for the number of out-of-home placements. Similarity

on spreads of the scatter plots indicates homogeneity of variance.

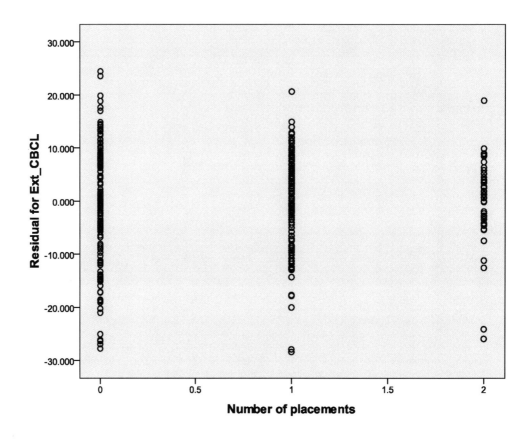

Figure 4.28. Scatter plot of residuals of the Externalizing Behavior of the Child

Behavior Checklist (CBCL) for the number of out-of-home placements. Similarity

on spreads of the scatter plots indicates homogeneity of variance.

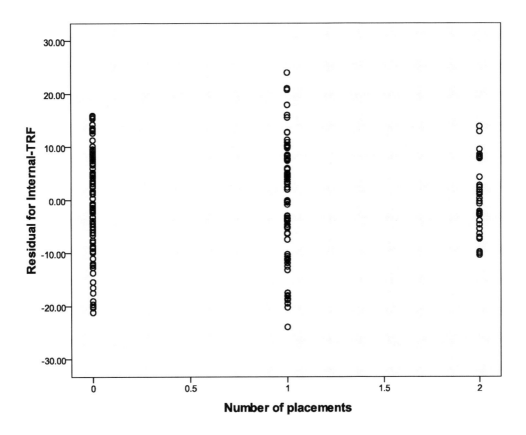

Figure 4.29. Scatter plot of residuals of the Internalizing Behavior of the Teacher Report Form (TRF) for the number of out-of-home placements. Similarity on spreads of the scatter plots indicates homogeneity of variance.

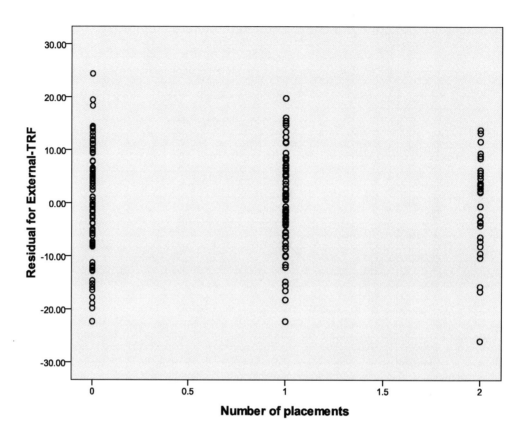

Figure 4.30. Scatter plot of residuals of the Externalizing Behavior of the Teacher

Report Form (TRF) for the number of out-of-home placements. Similarity on

spreads of the scatter plots indicates homogeneity of variance.

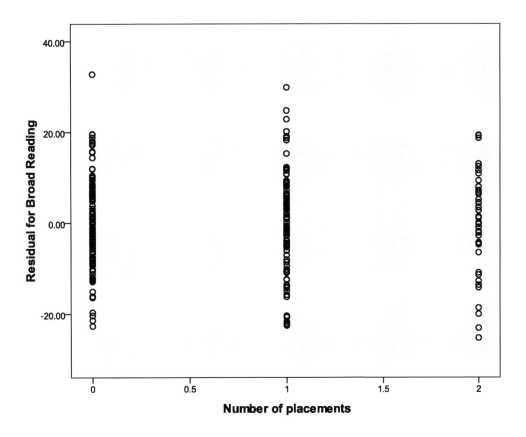

Figure 4.31. Scatter plot of residuals of the Broad Reading composite of the
Woodcock Johnson Test of Achievement- Third Edition (WJ III ACH) for the
number of out-of-home placements. Similarity on spreads of the scatter plots
indicates homogeneity of variance.

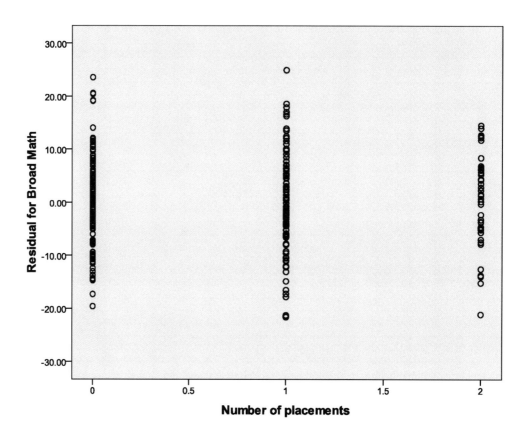

Figure 4.32. Scatter plot of residuals of the Broad Math composite of the

Woodcock Johnson Test of Achievement- Third Edition (WJ III ACH) for the

number of out-of-home placements. Similarity on spreads of the scatter plots

indicates homogeneity of variance.

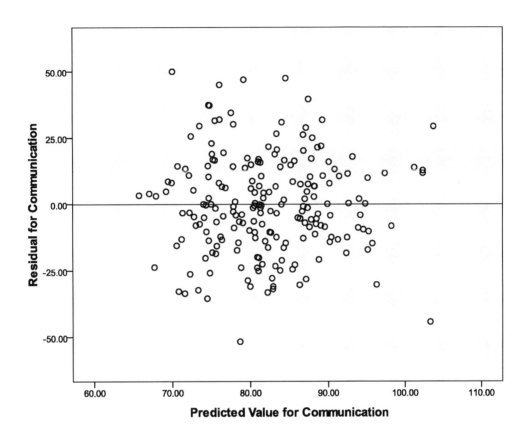

Figure 4.33 Scatter plot of residuals and predicted values of the Social

Interaction and Communication composite of the Scales of Independent

Behavior- Revised (SIB-R).

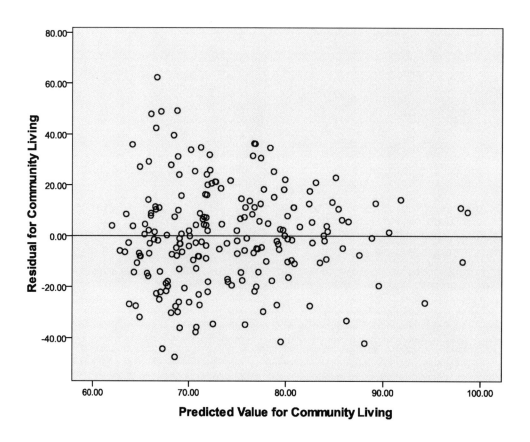

Figure 4.34. Scatter plot of residuals and predicted values of the Community

Living composite of the Scales of Independent Behavior- Revised (SIB-R).

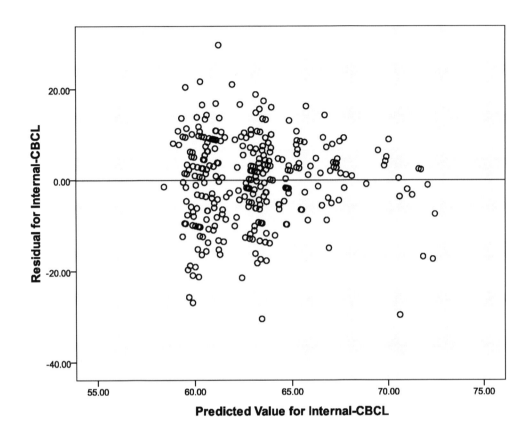

Figure 4.35. Scatter plot of residuals and predicted values of the Internalizing

Behavior of the Child Behavior Checklist (CBCL).

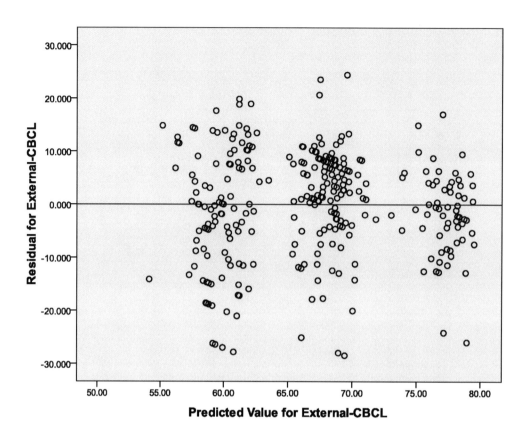

Figure 4.36. Scatter plot of residuals and predicted values of the Externalizing

Behavior of the Child Behavior Checklist (CBCL).

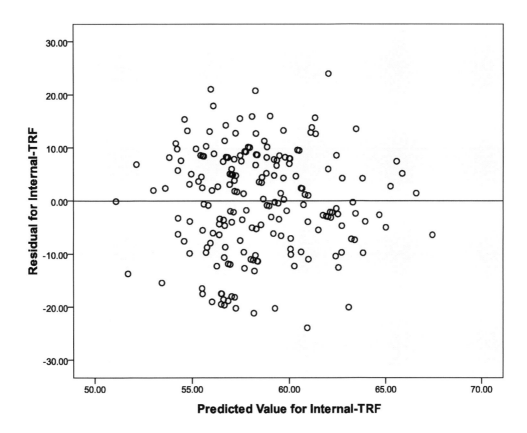

Figure 4.37. Scatter plot of residuals and predicted values of the Internalizing

Behavior of the Teacher Report Form (TRF).

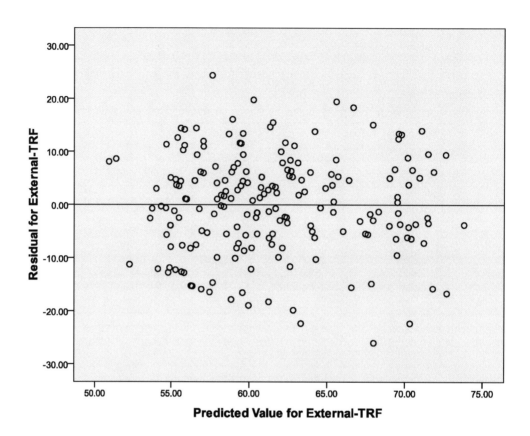

Figure 4.38. Scatter plot of residuals and predicted values of the Externalizing

Behavior of the Teacher Report Form (TRF).

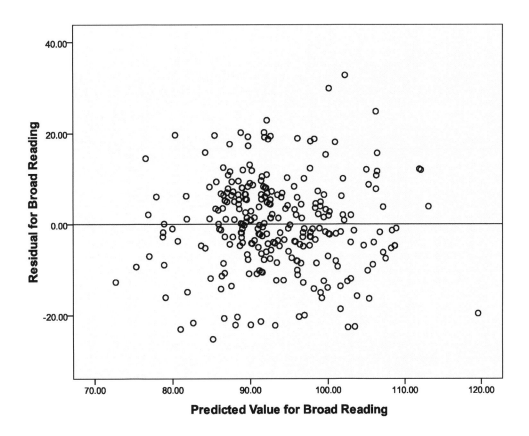

Figure 4.39. Scatter plot of residuals and predicted values of the Broad Reading composite of the Woodcock Johnson Test of Achievement- Third Edition (WJ III ACH).

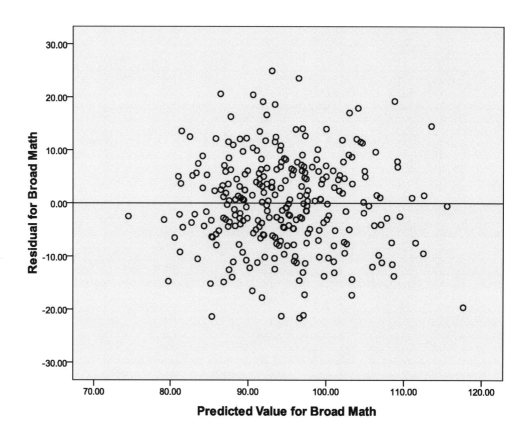

Figure 4.40. Scatter plot of residuals and predicted values of the Broad Math

composite of the Woodcock Johnson Test of Achievement- Third Edition (WJ III

ACH).

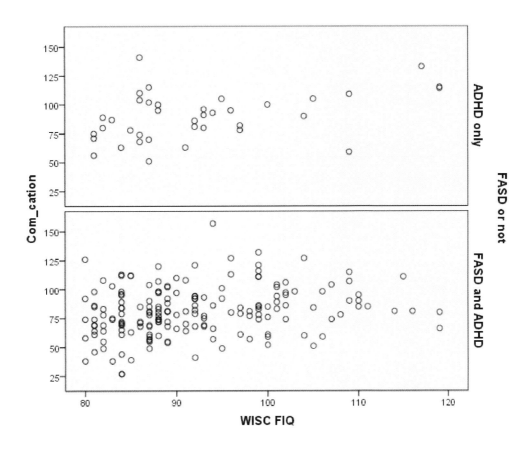

Figure 4.41. Trends of the scatter plots of the Social Interaction and

Communication composite of the Scales of Independent Behavior- Revised (SIB-

R) for full-scale IQ (FSIQ) by the single diagnosis group and the dual diagnosis

group. A match on trends of the scatter plots of the two groups indicates

homogeneity of regression.

139

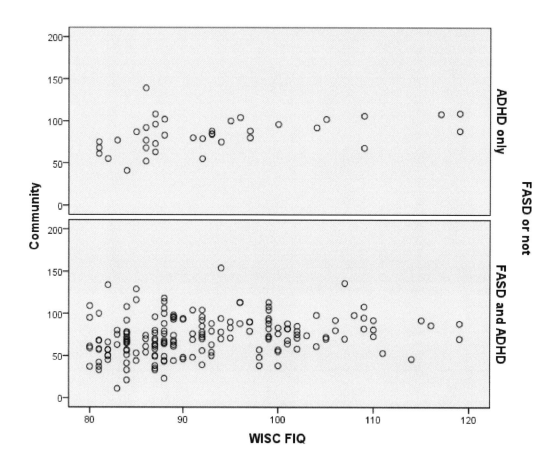

Figure 4.42. Trends of the scatter plots of the Community Living composite of the

Scales of Independent Behavior- Revised (SIB-R) for full-scale IQ (FSIQ) by the

single diagnosis group and the dual diagnosis group. A match on trends of the

scatter plots of the two groups indicates homogeneity of regression.

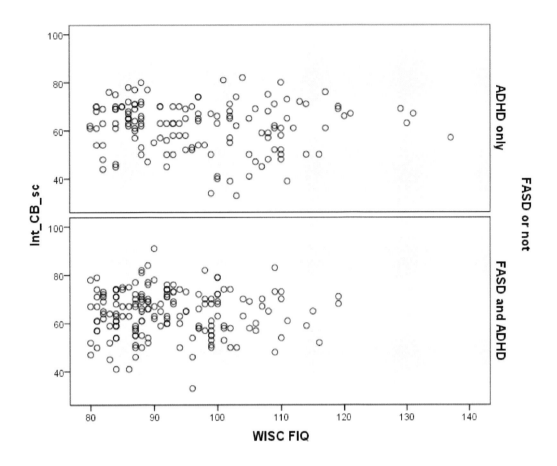

Figure 4.43. Trends of the scatter plots of the Internalizing Behavior of the Child

Behavior Checklist (CBCL) for full-scale IQ (FSIQ) by the single diagnosis group

and the dual diagnosis group. A match on trends of the scatter plots of the two

groups indicates homogeneity of regression.

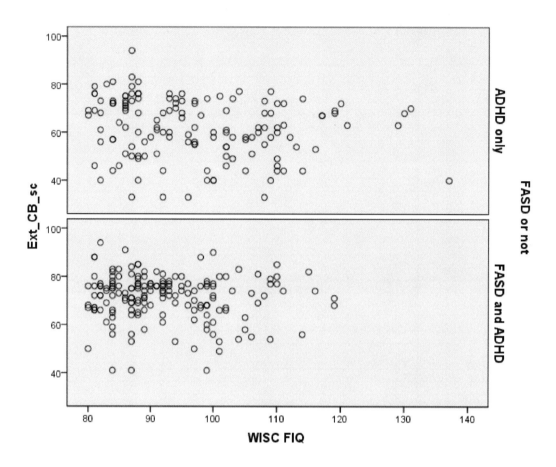

Figure 4.44. Trends of the scatter plots of the Externalizing Behavior of the Child Behavior Checklist (CBCL) for full-scale IQ (FSIQ) by the single diagnosis group and the dual diagnosis group. A match on trends of the scatter plots of the two groups indicates homogeneity of regression.

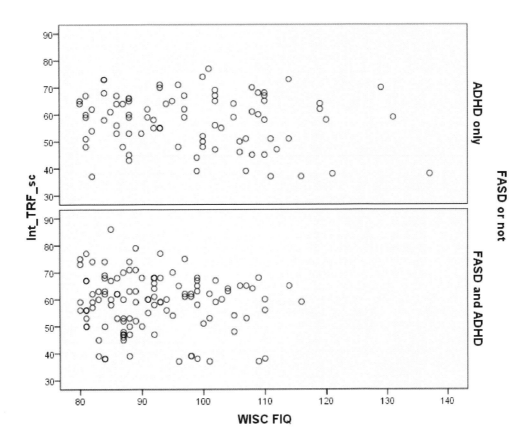

Figure 4.45. Trends of the scatter plots of the Internalizing Behavior of the

Teacher Report Form (TRF) for full-scale IQ (FSIQ) by the single diagnosis group

and the dual diagnosis group. A match on trends of the scatter plots of the two

groups indicates homogeneity of regression.

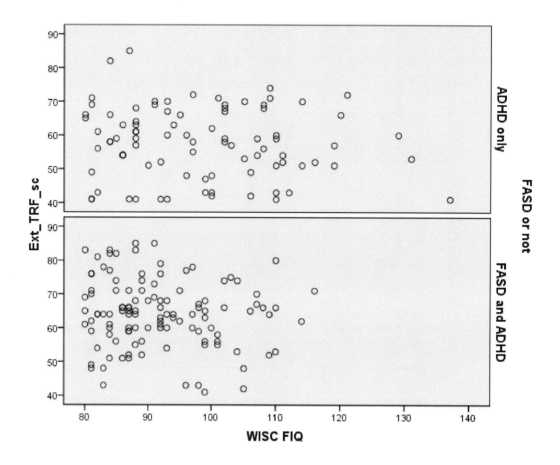

Figure 4.46. Trends of the scatter plots of the Externalizing Behavior of the

Teacher Report Form (TRF) for full-scale IQ (FSIQ) by the single diagnosis group

and the dual diagnosis group. A match on trends of the scatter plots of the two

groups indicates homogeneity of regression.

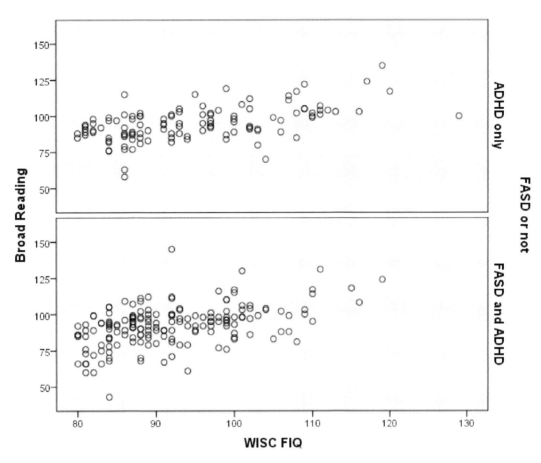

Figure 4.47. Trends of the scatter plots of the Broad Reading composite of the Woodcock Johnson Test of Achievement- Third Edition (WJ III ACH) for full-scale IQ (FSIQ) by the single diagnosis group and the dual diagnosis group. A match on trends of the scatter plots of the two groups indicates homogeneity of regression.

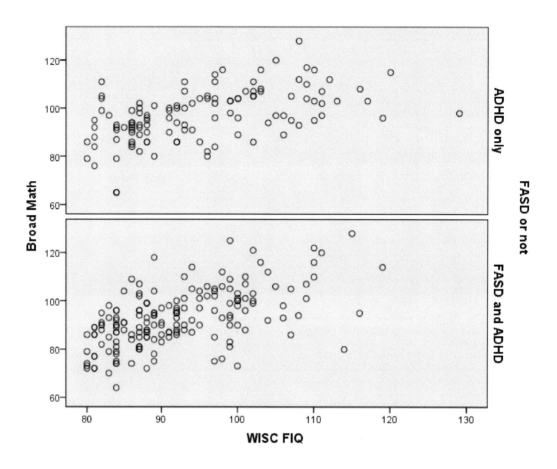

Figure 4.48. Trends of the scatter plots of the Broad Math composite of the

Woodcock Johnson Test of Achievement- Third Edition (WJ III ACH) for full-scale

IQ (FSIQ) by the single diagnosis group and the dual diagnosis group. A match

on trends of the scatter plots of the two groups indicates homogeneity of

regression.

146

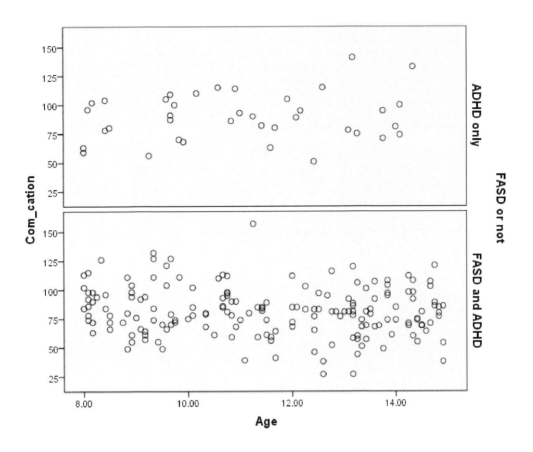

Figure 4.49. Trends of the scatter plots of the Social Interaction and Communication composite of the Scales of Independent Behavior- Revised (SIB-R) for age by the single diagnosis group and the dual diagnosis group. A match on trends of the scatter plots of the two groups indicates homogeneity of regression.

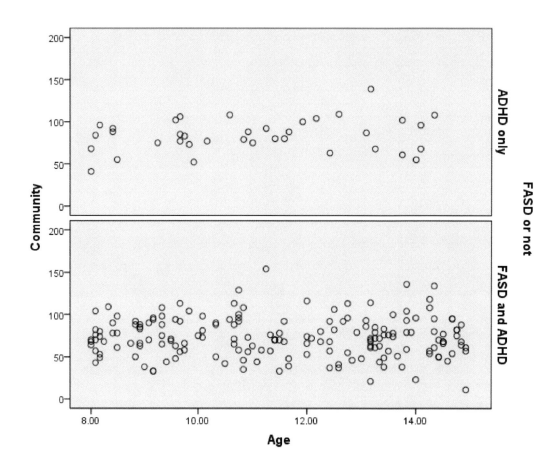

Figure 4.50. Trends of the scatter plots of the Community Living composite of the

Scales of Independent Behavior- Revised (SIB-R) for age by the single diagnosis

group and the dual diagnosis group. A match on trends of the scatter plots of the

two groups indicates homogeneity of regression.

148

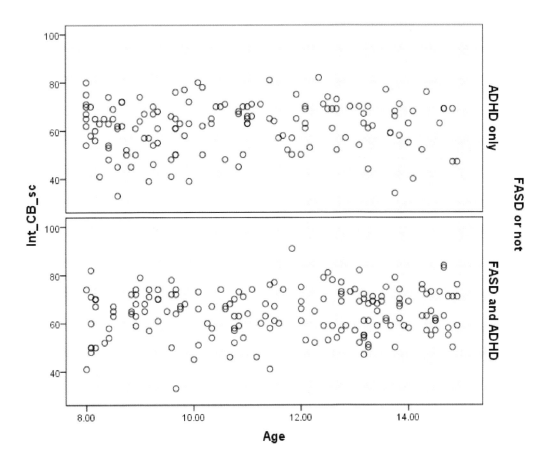

Figure 4.51. Trends of the scatter plots of the Internalizing Behavior of the Child

Behavior Checklist (CBCL) for age by the single diagnosis group and the dual

diagnosis group. A match on trends of the scatter plots of the two groups

indicates homogeneity of regression.

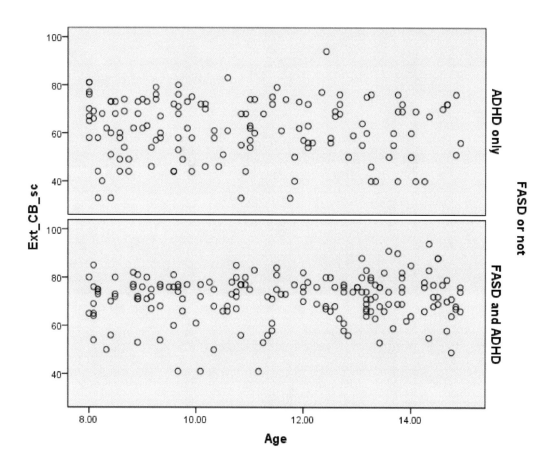

Figure 4.52. Trends of the scatter plots of the Externalizing Behavior of the Child

Behavior Checklist (CBCL) for age by the single diagnosis group and the dual

diagnosis group. A match on trends of the scatter plots of the two groups

indicates homogeneity of regression.

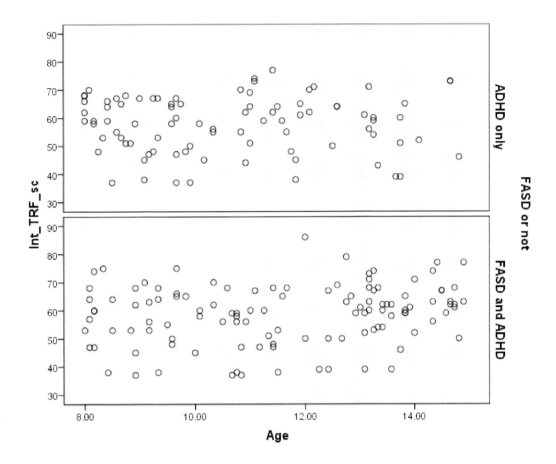

Figure 4.53. Trends of the scatter plots of the Internalizing Behavior of the

Teacher Report Form (TRF) for age by the single diagnosis group and the dual

diagnosis group. A match on trends of the scatter plots of the two groups

indicates homogeneity of regression.

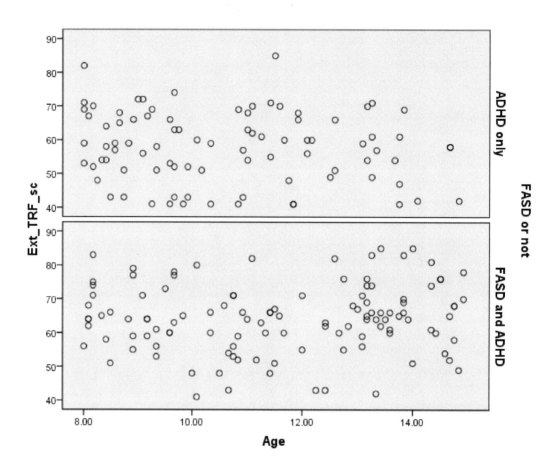

Figure 4.54. Trends of the scatter plots of the Externalizing Behavior of the

Teacher Report Form (TRF) for age by the single diagnosis group and the dual

diagnosis group. A match on trends of the scatter plots of the two groups

indicates homogeneity of regression.

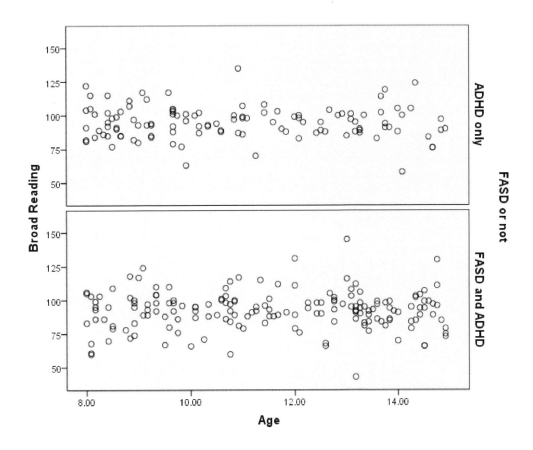

Figure 4.55. Trends of the scatter plots of the Broad Reading composite of the Woodcock Johnson Test of Achievement- Third Edition (WJ III ACH) for age by the single diagnosis group and the dual diagnosis group. A match on trends of the scatter plots of the two groups indicates homogeneity of regression.

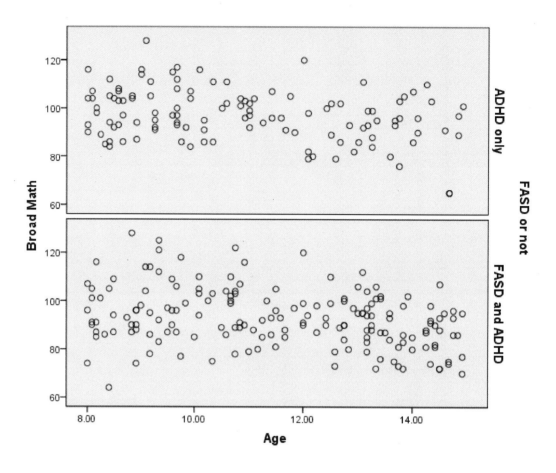

Figure 4.56. Trends of the scatter plots of the Broad Math composite of the Woodcock Johnson Test of Achievement- Third Edition (WJ III ACH) for age by the single diagnosis group and the dual diagnosis group. A match on trends of the scatter plots of the two groups indicates homogeneity of regression.